Damaged Merchandise

Elaine D. Marsh

&

Damaged Merchandise
By Elaine D. Marsh

Copyright 2021 by Elaine D. Marsh
Cover Copyright 2019 by Untreed Reads Publishing
Cover Design by Ginny Glass

ISBN-13: 978-0-578-83697-3

Also available in ebook format.

Published by Elaine D. Marsh
damagedmerchandise8@gmail.com

Printed in the United States of America.

Note
All names have been changed in the writing of this story, for the privacy of the individuals.

Dedicated to Susan, my husband,
my daughter and my son.

Damaged Merchandise

Elaine D. Marsh

1

I am 17 years old and I feel very sick, dizzy, disoriented and nauseous. My mother and I are sitting at the kitchen table together right after she has spoken with Dr. Snyder, my shrink, and I can see the wheels spinning in her head about how she can manipulate the situation to fit with her agenda of going to the wedding. She looks at me and says, "I'm sure you are going to be just fine, let's go to Indiana anyway." I don't remember if she even discussed it with my father. I don't think so. She made all the decisions. So, off we go to Fort Wayne, Indiana. I know this is a bad idea.

It is a four-hour drive from our home in Michigan. We wait for my dad to get home from work. We are ready to leave when he walks in the door. We pack the car and off we go. It is just me, my mother and my father on this short weekend trip.

My father drives the whole way. We are in my mother's Buick LaSabre. That is the only kind of car she drives. She trades it in every three years. It is green with a green vinyl top. And the windows in the back seat do not go down all the way. They only go down halfway, lucky for me. Not so lucky for my parents. I think they are trying to kill me. The lithium is doing its thing. It appears that I am having a toxic reaction to the dosage I am on. Kind of like overdosing, but not because I want to get high; no, because my mother and the shrink want to have control over me. The shrink says I am manic depressive.

I am in the back seat wearing a sweater that I handmade, myself. Knitting is relaxing for me, also an escape; my grandmother taught me how to knit when I was four. It is a wheat color, long, past my waist, no collar, with a basket weave stitch. Four stitches of knitting and four stitches of pearling and then alternating every four rows, to get a checkerboard effect.

I am still in the back seat, but I am not myself. I am afraid, nervous that more is going to go wrong. I do not feel safe with my parents. I need to get away from them. No doubt, I am starting to hallucinate from the toxic reaction I am having from the lithium, but of course, I don't know that's what is happening. I need to escape. I put the backseat window down as far as it will go and try to jump out the window. My father is driving on the highway at 70 miles per hour. My mother screams when she realizes what is going on and tries to climb over the front seat and stop me. She isn't successful at getting over the seat, but I am not successful at getting out the window either. I don't fit through the opening.

*

Sometime later we arrive at the hotel, a Holiday Inn. My father needs to rest from his day, and at this point my mother finally knows I am too sick to attend the wedding. We will stay in the room for the night so that my father can rest, and we will drive home in the morning. I have a bad gut feeling I am in big trouble. My parents have plans to kill me tonight. I am sure of that.

This is how I have come to this conclusion. My mother is a great saver when it comes to money, especially if she is saving money for something she wants. She wants a two-carat diamond ring for her 25th wedding anniversary to my father. She has saved for many years and now has $10,000. The year is 1972 and this is a lot of money. She and my father picked out the diamond; it is a pear shape. The jeweler picked out the first setting. The diamond is deep set, and in this setting you cannot see the many beautiful facets it has. My mother hates the setting. She picks out the next setting, and after going to pick it up, still does not like that one any better. She says it is too heavy and will not be comfortable. She and the jeweler put their heads together to come up with one more setting for the huge diamond. But she has to leave it with him again.

She does not have the ring when we leave for Indiana. This upsets her; she *says* she really wants to show it off to her family. But I am sure that my mother is not having her diamond reset again, and instead has gotten her $10,000 back to hire a gunman to kill me. I am a problem and they need to get rid of me. I am sure of that!

My mother calls Dr. Snyder when we get to the hotel room. I can hear him through the phone. He is scolding my mother for taking me out of town. When they had a conversation earlier Dr. Snyder was clear about not taking me out of town. He told her not to. She has an agenda. It suits her to take me. What matters is her getting rid of me.

The hotel room is laid out so that when you walk through the door, the bathroom is on the right side. Beyond the bathroom on the right, two queen-size beds take up the whole room. When I walk into the bathroom the sink is on the right, the toilet in the middle and the bathtub and shower curtain on the left. The shower curtain is a solid color, beige; you cannot see through it, it is not transparent, not at all.

Across from the bathroom is a door that connects to the room next door. We did not rent that room, but the door exists for someone who wants to rent both rooms at one time and make them a connecting room. Possibly a large family who needs two rooms and will leave the connecting door open during their stay at the hotel. That is not the case for us; we only need one room that night, just one room.

It is late and we are going to sleep. I am in a bed by myself and start to hear the doorknob move from the connecting room next to ours. I am sure of it, very sure. I tell my mother. She tells me to be quiet, that my dad needs his sleep so he can drive us home in the morning. I keep hearing the knob turning, and it is very scary. I break out in a sweat and start to scream. Next thing I know is that my mother has left the bed she is in next to the window with my father and is holding me in my bed.

I tell her I have to go to the bathroom. She says fine and I get up to walk there. I hear rustling of the shower curtain and am sure the gunman is behind the curtain. I run back to the bed and tell my mother. She tells me to stop being silly and to go back to the bathroom myself. I start sobbing and tell her no. My mother finally says she will go with me. I shake the whole time.

We leave the bathroom together and my mother and I get back into my bed. The wall next to my bed is the same wall that the shower is on. I can't sleep, that is impossible. I can barely breathe. As a matter of fact, I don't want to breathe, so that the killer in the bathroom, the gunman, will not hear me, find me and kill me.

I know I am not going to make it out of the hotel room alive. At some point during the night my mother is going to force me to return to the bathroom alone so that the deed can be done. Once and for all they will be rid of me.

I keep hearing noise from the bathroom, from the shower. I am frozen with fear. My mother cannot understand why. I can't share it with her. She is part of the plan. If I let her know that I am aware of what she and my father are up to, I will be a goner that much sooner. Maybe there is a way out for me. Maybe I can escape through the connecting door?

As the night goes on, I get worse and worse. The toxicity is taking over, the hallucinations are getting worse. They are becoming more real and intense. It is a living hell. I am sweating profusely.

My mother keeps telling me to go into the bathroom and get a towel to wipe the sweat. I refuse. Eventually, she gets a towel for me. I can still hear the rustling in the shower; he is waiting, waiting for the right minute to shoot me. Does he have a silencer on the gun, like you see in the movies? Otherwise someone is bound to hear the gun go off. And my parents certainly don't want to be found guilty of any wrongdoings. It really will ruin my mother's agenda.

I am sure she has already come up with a lie, some story that the man with the gun comes through the connecting door to rob them, and that there is a struggle between the gunman and my father and the gun goes off. I am the casualty. I am the one who gets shot by accident, and I am dead. Low and behold the gunman escapes and is never caught. The job is done. I am gone, dead, out of their hair for good.

After a never-ending night, the daylight finally begins to show through the drapes. I did not get any sleep. I am not sure anyone did. I know the assassin is still in the shower waiting for the opportunity to kill me.

*

I don't have many memories after that point. Not getting any sleep, not eating anything. My body is fighting the toxic reaction to the lithium is too much. The hallucinations continue but they become hazy.

My mother has another conversation with Dr. Snyder the morning we are leaving the hotel. After she shares the events of the evening with him, he is sure I am having a serious lithium toxicity reaction and he instructs her to bring me right to the hospital. Not to go anywhere first. To drive straight to the hospital and make it fast.

2

I have no recollection of the ride back home. I do remember arriving at the hospital. My parents take me inside. The nurses have specific instructions of how to handle me as soon as I get there. I am not steady on my feet, having trouble walking, and my father is helping me. There is a big, bad-looking male nurse who says he has an injection ready for me. I don't want an injection. Isn't it bad enough that the lithium is causing hallucinations and my parents hire an assassin?

I am no match for the big, bad male nurse, and my parents certainly are not on my side. They must have been thinking that since the gunman had not been successful in killing me, here is another chance for them to get rid of me. Who knows what is in the syringe, something that will do the trick, lights out for good?

The last thing I remember is the needle going into my right arm and how forceful the male nurse is, and how much it hurts and how much he does not care. Everything goes pitch black.

*

Whether I am sleeping, given drugs and in a stupor, or am even a coma, it turns out that this is a psychiatric hospital. I am suffering from hallucinations from a toxic reaction to a psychotropic drug that I find out later in my life I actually did not need—and my organs may have been shutting down. What I need is medical help, but, yes, instead, they have taken me to a psychiatric hospital—because that is what Dr. Snyder told my mother to do, she agreed…and my father almost always does what my mother wants.

What I remember most about this psychiatric hospital is being in a room with a lock on the outside, no way out. On the floor with a hospital gown tied at my back and neck. The staff coming in to give me more injections. And I sleep. I do not remember eating at all or even ever going to the bathroom.

*

My father picks me up a few days later and takes me to another hospital, for observation. This is a regular hospital, but it has a psych unit as well. My father tells me that I have been in a drug-induced coma, from the lithium toxicity and from the injectable drugs they have been giving me to keep me quiet. I have very little recollection of my stay at the first psychiatric hospital.

At the new hospital an endocrinologist, Dr. Burger, orders further testing when I arrive there; lots of testing—lots of testing with iodine, which proves to be an almost fatal mistake, which I find out some thirty years later.

* * *

How did I—and my mother—get to this frightening and "out of control" place in my life? *Control.* What follows is the story of how my mother's obsessive need for it—and inability to always have it—resulted in a life full of hellish moments for a substantial part of my life. How her choices set me up for a lifetime of life-threatening illnesses I continue to face today. And how me taking back control has allowed me to survive and flourish, despite my body continually fighting against me.

My mother made so many decisions about my care that were about as bad as they could have been. She had a hard childhood herself, and I would have thought that would have made it even more important to her to take care of me. Unfortunately, that was not the case.

Our stories began innocently enough—as most people's stories often do. Our story demonstrates how events, personalities—and choices—shape the future. My mother's choices threatened—and still threaten—my life. But *my* choices brought me to a life of survival, yes, but so far beyond that—beyond the fear, beyond the challenges…to a life filled with joy and happiness, finally breaking the cycle she and my grandmother started. My passion is to help others not go through the things I have had to survive.

Here is my story…which begins with her story.

3

My mother is the only girl in her family. She has three older brothers and one younger one. The apple of her father's eye, my mother still had a tough time growing up. She sometimes admits it. My grandmother was a handful. And being the only daughter made it harder on my mother. She had to take responsibility for helping my grandmother more than she would have liked. My mother was a bit of a tomboy and resented having to help around the house. I didn't know until I was in my early thirties that my grandmother was suicidal when she was raising her five children. My Papa would have to hire someone to watch her at night so he could sleep. A lot of this responsibility also fell on my mother during the day after school, which affected her deeply, leaving her extremely self-centered to say the least.

As hard as life could be for my mother, there were also examples of how she was loved by her family.

As a teenager, my mother needed braces on her teeth, and my grandparents said they had enough money for only one child to have braces. My Uncle Simon was the oldest, so he was the one that was going to get the braces. He was a real sport and said the girl in the family should have them. Amazing that my grandparents agreed, but they did. My mother took a bus to the orthodontist office for four years until the process was complete.

She also took piano lessons. Something I was very envious of. She again took the bus to the piano teacher's house for lessons weekly for several years. She never played the piano after her lessons. Maybe it had something to do with the fact that there was not a piano at her house to practice on. She says she was tone deaf and didn't like to play.

A lot of her friends and family called her "Slugger." She and all of her siblings would go to overnight camp for three weeks every summer. My mother loved it and that is where she got the nickname. She was a tomboy and loved to play ball with her brothers.

Lucky for her she had the opportunity to go to overnight camp. The camp was on a lake with many activities; there was canoeing, hiking through nature trails, crafts, and baseball too. She met Ellen there. Ellen was her counselor and my mother adored her.

Ellen was more of a mentor than a friend to my mother. When my mother got her period for the first time, she was at home and my grandfather congratulated her and told her she was a woman now. She had not wanted to approach her mother, afraid she might get in trouble. My mother had no clue what a period was, how often it would occur, or what to expect. Ellen was the one who made it easier for my mother. My mother would call Ellen and ask her all sorts of questions to help her through her teenage years.

*

After my mother graduated from high school, she and three of her closest friends went on a trip to a beach town in Michigan. They had a memorable time, and this is where my mother met my father. My mother tells the story that she was dating Henry Kimball at the time, but after meeting my father it was all over with Henry.

They were both 19 and my father said it was love at first sight. My father was very romantic and wrote my mother poems about love and happiness. I still have copies of a few of them. They did not date for very long before they became engaged; however, my grandmother was struggling with depression again, and it didn't look like she would be able to plan a wedding anytime soon.

My parents decided to get married by the justice of the peace at the courthouse. My mother wore a suit, and my father bought her lovely flowers to pin to her lapel. They did not take a honeymoon, as World War II was starting.

*

My father had enlisted in the army and would be traveling to many different US cities for training. He spoke several languages, and was going to be a translator. He would be stationed in many cities before he would be assigned a permanent position in Europe during WW II. Since my parents were married, my mother was able to tag along, and would always find a job where my father was training. The way my mother describes their travels on the troop trains, it sounds like they had a lot of fun together. Especially since they had both left behind oppressive environments. She was no longer on suicide watch for her mother and getting away from that had to be very freeing.

*

My father was the oldest of three children; he had a younger sister and brother. His parents had an arranged marriage and hadn't shared a bedroom for decades. My father worked for his father for years and was promised he would be paid for his hard work but never was. He helped his mother often around the house as his father was basically useless. My dad worked two jobs to put himself through college. He graduated early from high school and was just graduated from college at age 20 when the war broke out.

When my dad had to go to Europe, my mother returned home to her parents' house. She says she took up knitting, which is hard to believe. I know she also had a job; usually they were bookkeeper positions. She and her friends would go to the movies every weekend, and my father would send home money to his mother to buy an orchid corsage for my mother, this went on for several months. All her friends were jealous. My mother, being practical and a saver, finally told my father to save the money and not send it home for orchids.

My father sent my mother this poem on their second anniversary:

May 23, 1945
2nd Anniversary

Of all the days throughout the year
Today's one with special meaning, dear.

To say I love you seems so very mild,
For you're my every life—Over whom I'm wild!
So please always remember, my dear
Keep faith and lay aside all fear
The sun will shine once more
To warm our hearts to the very core!
Today's two years to the very date
That I can proudly, say you've been my mate
Smile, my angel—across the wide cruel space
And join in my prayer that a full life will be ours to taste.

Eternally,
Sam

*

My father was a translator during WW II. He spoke Spanish, French, German and English. Because my father did not know how to drive a car, nor have a driver's license for that matter, he had a chauffeur who would drive him from place to place in an army Jeep. It made him look like an officer, but he had no desire to make the army his career and wanted to get home to my mother as quickly as possible and start a family.

With his job as a translator, he was often in tough situations. He would have to go into concentration camps to translate as the war was ending. He would help the survivors of the war communicate with the US Army to help get them to a better place.

My dad could have become an officer, but he wasn't interested in making the army his career. He was most interested in getting home to my mother and starting a family.

*

It was a joyous day when my dad came home from the war. My parents were ready to move into the four-flat that my Papa, my mother's father, had bought for his four eldest children as a surprise when they arrived back on United States soil. All my uncles came back unharmed. At least physically that is.

Since my mother had been diagnosed with a tumor on an ovary, and had a tube and ovary removed before having any of us, her obstetrician suggested they move along quickly with starting a family. He wasn't sure it would be that easy for her to conceive.

In the meantime, my parents were having fun furnishing their apartment. My dad's mother, Paula, bought them a kitchen set. My mother insisted on six chairs because she was planning on having four children.

Mom got pregnant pretty quickly with her first. Lee was born in May of 1948. He was an adorable baby, the best looking one of all of us. He resembled my mother's side of the family. Miles arrived in November of 1951, on a bitter cold afternoon. Miles was cute and sweet. He needed glasses at an early age for a lazy eye. Warren was born in April of 1954. He was a colicky baby and gave my mother a lot of trouble. He never slept through the night until he was way over a year old. I remember that his hair grew straight up, so Mom would always have to take him for a brush cut.

Lee and Miles had always gotten along just fine until Warren came along, then everything changed. Miles was now the middle child, and Miles and Warren became close and left Lee out.

Mom still couldn't believe she had three children successfully in six years, and she decided to wait a while to try for the fourth. And the fourth one had to be a girl. Even though Papa kept reminding her it wouldn't be possible for her to have a girl, because he believed that the female determined the sex, and after mom had a tube and ovary removed she would only be able to have boys. This seemed to be what people thought at the time. Mom wanted to have the fourth child anyway. Keeping in mind she had the kitchen chairs for it.

I was due to be born in early January 1958. When my mother's water broke on an evening late in December, she and my Dad where thrilled. It would mean that I would be born in 1957 instead of 1958, which would be cause for celebration. I would be a tax deduction!

My mother didn't believe I was a girl and insisted that my Dad remove my diaper. When her best friend sent pink carnations; she knew that was a sign it must be true as well. She got her girl!

They brought me home from the hospital and showed me off to my brothers. My brothers were not sure what to do with me. My mother acted as if I would break.

4

I think my mother's and father's lives were fairly happy for the next few years, but when I was 2½ years old my mother's father, my beloved Papa, died. Looking back, I realize this is when my mother's personality seemed to change—not for the good. It was as if her father dying "broke her." I remember lying in bed with her sometimes with her just crying with grief. My mother already had a stern and controlling personality and unfortunately, from then on, it got worse…especially for me.

*

In 1948 we moved into the first house my parents owned after leaving the four-flat.

I often wonder why we had to have plastic covers on our furniture. I ask my mother that and she tells me that everyone who buys new furniture invests in plastic covers, so that the furniture will always be new underneath the plastic. I don't like the plastic at all. I stick to the couch or chair when I sit on them. It doesn't feel good at all. Sometimes I have red marks on the back of my legs that sting. That is why I sit on the floor more often than not.

Then there are the draperies. They are a linen fabric with large red flowers on them, along with greens. They are custom-made at the local drapery shop. We have a large picture window in the living room that has drapes with the same pattern as the dining room drapes. But I can't figure it out. When I am outside walking home from school with Warren, we walk up to the house and I can see the lining of the drapes from the sidewalk. It is beige, plain beige.

I ask my mother why it is like that. She has no idea what I am talking about, so I explain. I tell her I don't understand why you can't see the pretty side of the drapes from the outside of the house. Isn't that the side that people get to see when approaching our house? She laughs for a long time and then takes me onto her lap and explains that the pretty side of the drapes with the big red flowers and green leaves are for all of us to enjoy inside the house. I feel stupid, but she is very patient.

I'm glad I have this memory, because these kinds of moments had been fewer and fewer in recent years. And as I got older and my health problems arose, "patient" is not a word I would use to describe my mother. She seemed to not want to be bothered having to "deal with me."

There is a two-car garage behind the house that does not connect to the house. Someone put a basketball hoop over the garage doors. I am pretty sure my Dad did not install it; he really is not too handy with tools. Lee, Warren and I have that talent. We all love playing basketball together, even though it seems that it is never my turn to have the ball. It does not really matter to me. I love spending time with my brothers, no matter what we are doing.

Warren and I also play catch in the backyard or the driveway. I use Lee's mitt, which puts me at a disadvantage, as it keeps falling off my hand. But it is still fun.

There is a door leading out of the kitchen that goes to a stairway, down to our basement. I enjoy our basement. The walls have a wood finish on them, and we all play games together down there, like hide and go seek, hot potato and musical chairs to name a few. We also have a table to do jigsaw puzzles on. Working on the puzzles with my dad are my favorite times. Life is so wonderful with my dad. He is loving and patient and wants to spend time with me.

There is this great big closet in my bedroom. On the floor there are pieces of wood, which are as long as the closet is wide, with a rack on the floor to lean shoes on, and above that, there is a long round pole to hang clothes from.

Some of my mother's friends and our family give me custom-made dresses from Margo's as gifts. It turns out that my mother just loves looking at them, and looking at them on a regular basis. I have the prettiest party dresses, all on silk hangers. The dresses are in every color you can imagine, pale pink and lavender, sky blue, bright orange, red and florals too. She takes them out of my closet, holds them up to me and says, "This one looks like it might fit you soon!" I never get to wear any of them; she only holds them up to me and goes on about how beautiful they will look on me. It makes me sad that I don't even get to try on the dresses for fun. My mom says we don't want to wrinkle them.

My mother was brought up during the great depression. She had a habit of saving things until they were too small to wear, as if she somehow was not worthy or deserving to wear the clothing. She tells the story of the time my Papa bought her a pair of green and pink polka-dot flannel pajamas. She loved those pajamas and would look at them all the time. By the time my mother decided to wear the pajamas they were too small.

This means that once again the special handmade dresses from Margo's are not going to be something I wear. It is unclear when there will be an event for a special dress.

When I am 6, the dresses from Margo's shop no longer fit me. I believe being the type of person that my mother is she will arrange for Margo to refund her for the dresses.

*

One night, my parents are nowhere to be found and I am watching TV by myself. *Outer Limits*, a science fiction TV program, is ending and next a movie is coming on, *The Snake Pit* with Oliva de Haviland. The movie is in black and white and the main character, Olivia, has been committed to a state psychiatric ward by her husband. The camera zooms in and it looks like an actual pit, where people are swarming around, horrifying. Why am I left alone to watch this, no supervision? *Is this a sign of what is to come?*

*

I also remember many happy times at that house, getting into mischief, and playing with my brothers in our backyard. One day when I am 3, we are in our backyard playing on the swing set, you

17

know, the kind that is metal and is dug into the ground usually with cement to hold it in place. Well, ours isn't secure with cement, and on one of our big swings forward, the swing set lifts out of the ground as Warren and I go flying toward the house.

We both end up landing close to the back porch and checking each other to be sure we are fine. I don't even cry until I realize that the swing set has fallen on top of the lilies of the valley in the garden bed near the back porch. They are my favorites, with the tiny white bells hanging from the long green stems. I run into the house to get my mother. She doesn't seem to care how upset I am about my favorite flowers; she is just mad that the swing set has come out of the ground and is now history. A few weeks later, the swing set ends up in the trash.

*

When I'm old enough for kindergarten, my brothers and I attend the same school, which has both an elementary and middle school. It is during the time when there are air raid drills. When the alarm sounds, off we go in an orderly fashion to the main building of the school, which has a basement. The students take some newspaper to sit on in the basement of the school.

The school basement walls have our classroom teachers' names, and we place our newspaper on the floor and sit on it and wait for further instructions. After fifteen to twenty minutes the alarm sounds again, and the teachers tell us it is safe to return to our classrooms and that the drill is over.

My first kindergarten teacher's name is Miss Lummis. I like her very much. She is kind, pretty and smart. Our class is held in a portable trailer. The school is too small to hold all the students, so they have portables for the kindergarten and first grade classes, similar to a mobile home, but with classrooms in them.

At one end of the classroom there is what looks like a wall, but when Miss Lummis pulls on one end, parts of the wall move, like an accordion. The wall is actually louver doors that hide hooks and cubbies behind it for our lunches and jackets.

I vividly remember—as most people my age and older do—Friday, November 22, 1963. In Dallas Texas, at 12:30 p.m., right before we are going home for the day, our president, John F. Kennedy, is shot in an assassination. The announcement comes over the P.A. system. Miss Lummis begins to cry, and the school has an early dismissal. This is very frightening, and many of us begin crying too.

*

Another time, soon after that, we have a half day of school. I walk to school each day with my brother Warren. My other brothers Lee and Miles are in junior high school at another campus. When class is over, right before lunch, I am waiting in the usual place by the front entrance of the school for Warren so we can walk home together as we always do. I wait and wait, and he never comes out, nor do any other students.

At that point, I decide to walk home myself. I know the way; it is about six blocks to my house. Three blocks towards the left of the school, when standing by the front door of the school, and then turn left for three blocks and ours is the house on the left halfway down the street.

I feel light and independent. I am a big girl. I can do this on my own. My mother will be so proud of me. As I walk away from the school grounds, a man walks up to me. A strange man, he is wearing a long black coat and a hat, similar to the kind of hat my dad wears. We all call it the "Bat Masterson" hat, just like on the TV show. The man asks me where I am going; don't I have school? I tell him that we only have half a day that day and I was waiting for a while for my brother Warren, but he must have a full day of school.

The man asks me if he can hold my hand, and it seems OK to me at the time. So off we go. I show him the way to my house. He is such a pleasant man, we talk about all the houses as we pass them, and I point out the ones of the people I know. When we are just about in front of my house, my mother runs out the front door screaming, "Take your hands of my baby! What are you doing with her?"

I am uneasy and can see that my mother is angry with me. She grabs me away from the man and scolds him. She pulls me into the house and scolds me as well. "Where is Warren?" she says. I tell her I don't know, but kindergarten and first grade have half a day, so I had to walk home alone, and the nice man walked with me.

Boy I am in big trouble. Don't I know not to talk to strangers? The man might try to kidnap me and kill me, and I am never to walk home from school alone again. Why didn't I go back to see Miss Lummis? I explain that after waiting for Warren at the main entrance of the school and realizing he isn't going to show up, I return to the portable, but it is already empty and Miss Lummis is nowhere in sight. My mother tells me if I do not find Warren ever again at our special place we meet, to go into the office in the school and ask someone inside to call home for me.

After yelling at me, my mother phones the school. As it turns out there was a flyer that came home from school reminding parents that there is a half day for kindergarten and first grade that day. Somehow my mother lost track of that notice.

5

At this time, my dad owns a 5 & Dime store. I love going there and looking at all the colorful things he has in the displays. School supplies; kitchen supplies, like aprons, towels, potholders, spatulas and spoons hanging on peg boards; sewing supplies; hardware items and toys. The toy department is my favorite. With Slinkys, bags of glass marbles, kites, paper dolls, pinwheels, cars, trucks and more.

But the very best part is the candy counter in the front of the store. Just inside the front door, on the left-hand side there are glass candy cases, full of chocolates, all in separate sections, for the chocolate-covered peanuts, raisins and cherries. There is a section for the nonpareils that have white sprinkles on top and are crunchy, and milk and dark chocolate chunks, caramels that melt in your mouth and those yummy turtles. Turtles are pecans and caramel dipped in milk chocolate.

When we all visit the store, Lee, Miles and Warren play hide and seek. Or at least that is what I think they are doing. It turns out that I find them behind the cases that hold the chocolates. Miles is lying on the floor with his mouth wide open. Lee is scooping chocolate-covered raisins out of the case and dropping them directly into his mouth. Warren wants to know when it is his turn. It is startling when they discover I am watching them and make me promise not to tell.

Next to the glass candy cases is a wall that has all the candies in packages: Boston Baked Beans, SweeTarts, Mallo Cups, Red Hots, Bit-O-Honey, Candy Buttons, Charleston Chews, Chuckles, Candy Cigarettes, Good & Plenty, Cinnamon Toothpicks, Wax Lips, Root Beer Barrels, Salt Water Taffy and much more.

My dad has Byron, the son of a family friend who is my age help him out at his 5 & Dime. Byron and I are going to be models. Dad sells Buster Brown clothes at the store and that is what we model. I wear a navy suit with a white blouse and bobby sox, with Keds sneakers, the ones that come with the decoding toy, that has

21

a clicker to make Morse code. Byron wears navy slacks, with a white shirt with a collar.

We pose on the counters in the store, where the Buster Brown clothing is on display, and also outside the store; standing next to each other, smiling for the camera. I am holding a pinwheel and have very short bangs with half my forehead showing, and Byron has his hands behind his back. We are really cute together.

6

When I am 5 years old, the whole family is getting ready for our first family vacation, all six of us—my mother, father, Lee, Miles, Warren and me. My brothers usually go to overnight camp in the summertime, but not this year. This trip is very exciting.

Our destination is Niagara Falls, in Ontario, Canada. It is a five-hour drive from our house. We all climb into "Betsy"—that is the name of our '57 Chevy. She is cream with turquoise. What a beauty.

After arriving in Canada, we bring in the luggage and check into the hotel. We unpack, freshen up and are off to dinner. As we are walking in the hallway to the dining room, we stop and look at an odd-looking machine. It turns out to be a small putting green, right there in the middle of the hallway.

My brothers especially want to try it out. They did and it is fun for them. What I enjoy is looking out the big picture windows on one side of the hallway that look directly down to Niagara Falls. We finally continue on to dinner and who do we bump into but Raymond Burr, the famous television attorney, Perry Mason! He looks even more foreboding in real life. He is a big man; the skin around his eyes is dark and reminds me of raccoons.

During this vacation, my mother complains about how hard it is to keep track of all of us. Along with how expensive it is to feed us three meals a day. My brothers and I have a great time, but it is clear that this will be the first and last time we all go on vacation together. My mother is sure of that.

7

Shortly after that vacation, there are two significant changes in our lives.

First, in 1964 we move to the suburbs—to a large subdivision that is under construction. All three model homes being built are colonials. Because my mother doesn't like to walk steps, she wants a ranch style home. During her pregnancy with my brother Warren, her legs swelled and remained that way after he was born. This is one of her excuses for not wanting to walk steps, besides being lazy.

My mother visits other subdivisions that are being built near ours and finds a ranch floor plan that she likes. She takes the plan to the developer of our subdivision. He agrees to use the plan to build us a house. He is happy to have another option for people who want to build a home with one floor, and he ends up using the floor plan several more times in our neighborhood.

By the way, at the new house, even though the backyard is big, my mother announces that it is too pretty to mess it up with a swing set.

My best friend Lynn's mother feels the same way about their backyard, so when we're older, Lynn and I use the swing set at the elementary school. Or we cut through neighbors' backyards and borrow their swing sets for a while. No one ever seems to mind. We often use the teeter-totter and sing the latest jingle from the Wesson Oil Commercial. It goes like this: "If you could see through yours like I could see through mine, then you'd be frying chicken just as light as mine!" We keep this a secret from our mothers that we are using neighbors' play areas.

*

My mother likes to do her shopping over the phone. This is before catalogs or online shopping. Her favorite store is Macy's. When she is looking for a specific item, one that she is already familiar with, a house dress for example, she will sit at her desk in the new house and call each Macy's store, until she finds the item she is looking for, then they will deliver it to our house. I always think it is odd that she will circle her finger around the inside of a can of paperclips while on the phone. This seems like an odd habit to me. Why does she do this? Does she have lots of nervous energy?

*

My parents make me a party for my 7th birthday in the basement. It is 1964 and this is my first party at our new house; upstairs is too fancy. My mom gets paper tablecloths, napkins, plates, cups, decorations and streamers for the party. The theme is The Jetsons. They are my favorites. We cover the ping pong table with the tablecloth and other items. Mom orders a cake with my name on it and pretty raspberry red and pink flowers.

Including me, there are ten kids there. It is a Saturday afternoon party and since my birthday is in late December, we have the party a week earlier, so that everyone will be available for it, with the coming holidays. We play pin the tail on the donkey, musical chairs and other fun games.

After making a wish and blowing out the candles, I open the presents. There is one that I love the most. It is a plush animal. A white dog that is sitting on all four legs with red ears; he is fluffy and cuddly all at the same time. I name him Red Ears. It is a gift from my new friend Jane.

Jane and I make potholders on looms and sell them door to door in our new neighborhood. Entrepreneurs in the making!

That evening I ask my mother if I can sleep with Red Ears. She gives me the standard answer. "No." I have never been able to sleep with plush animals. She thinks I will suffocate. I feel like a baby once again.

Once, and I mean one time only, my parents have my three brothers babysit for me. We have been living in the new house in the suburbs for a couple months. I don't know where my parents are going, but that doesn't matter. I am 6 Warren is 10, Miles is 13 and Lee is 16. Even though we all get along pretty well, when my parents go out it is like when "the cat is away the mice will play."

The minute my brothers hear the garage door close, the games begin. The three of them grab me, which isn't too difficult. They take me into the kitchen and turn on the water in the sink and then flip the switch for the garbage disposal. Next, they try unsuccessfully to put my feet down the disposal, while the disposal is running. I scream and cry and beg them to stop. Of course they never act this way to me when our mother is around!

First thing in the morning, I tell my mother what the boys did to me the night before. That is the last time all three of my brothers babysit for me. After that, Warren, who is closest in age to me, stays with me when my parents go out.

My parents' schedule is pretty predictable. Every other Wednesday evening they play gin rummy and poker. My dad plays with the same guys he went to kindergarten with. There are six of them. My mother plays with four other women who are married to the same guys my father plays poker with. My dad goes to one house and my mom goes to another for the games, and each time they meet they rotate houses where they meet. My mom always says that when the game is at our house, us kids were the only ones that stay in their rooms at bedtime and don't disturb the adults. That comment always makes us feel good.

On the nights that Warren and I are home alone. We often go into the kitchen and find where my mother stashes the Nestlé Crunch bars. We are always successful in finding them. The Nestlé Crunch bars have an inner layer of wax paper. We open the wax paper, leaving the candy bar on it and then place the wax paper on the heating vent on the floor of my bedroom. We wait for the crunch bar to melt. We love eating it when it melts.

*

— The second big change was with my dad's business. Based on my mother's reactions during that family vacation, my father realizes that the income from the 5 & Dime store isn't going to support four children. He discusses his thoughts with my mother, and she suggests he speak to her brothers, Simon and Paul, being that they own a lucrative hardware store.

Uncle Simon and Uncle Paul help my dad locate a hardware store. The owner of the hardware store wants to retire and is looking to sell his business. The building is not for sale and my father will have to lease the space. The location is about thirty minutes from our house. My father puts an offer on the business and soon it is his.

I am 6 years old when my father sells his 5 & Dime store. It happens quickly, and the move from one store to the other is seamless. He sells the store with all the merchandise. And he buys the hardware with all the merchandise as well. Business is good.

Dad enjoys his new business and business improves month after month for the first three years. So much so that he grows out of the space he is in. As it happens, the building across the parking lot becomes available. It is currently a grocery store that is moving to a larger location a mile away.

His lease is up at the current location. He puts in an offer on the building and soon is the proud owner of an empty, but large grocery store. One night soon after my father buys the building, the phone rings very early in the morning, 4:00 a.m. It is the fire department, calling to let my dad know that there has been a fire at the new location of his store.

The building burns to the ground. It is amazing that no one is hurt, and that because the building is empty, no merchandise has been lost, except for the shelving and displays. Fortunately, there is insurance on everything.

It takes about six months to rebuild. The insurance covers all the costs, along with the cost of new shelving and displays. My father gets a six-month extension on his lease at the old hardware store. He is able to oversee the construction of the new store, being that he is at the old store, still conducting business.

As soon as the four walls and roof are rebuilt. The displays arrive. It is my brothers and me who build the units. It is fun working together as a team. It takes a full month to assemble and arrange all the displays.

I am now 10 and I learn how to sew, but do not have a sewing machine at home. For my hard work at the store, my dad gives me a Brother sewing machine and console. The sewing machine is brown with pinkish coral in color, and when I am not using it, it folds inside a console and looks just like a piece of furniture. I am so thrilled about having my own sewing machine.

There is one thing from the old store that my dad brings with him to the new store, a nail carousel. It stands eight feet tall. It has five layers and they move, spin around, so you can see what is in each section. Each layer has six sections. Each section holds large nails. It has green paint on the whole thing, green just like an evergreen tree. I spin it for hours.

*

It is the mid-sixties, and my brothers and I gather around the TV in the family room for the first episode of *Batman*. Lee, Miles, Warren and I are all there. This is a big event. *Batman* is on twice a week, and that is where you will find us. I don't remember many other things that all four of us enjoy so much. As we grow older, we grow apart.

8

Summers after that are full of other activities. My brothers go to the same overnight camp that my mother and her brothers went to for many years. (When they are too old to be campers, they become counselors at the same camp.) I go to day camp close to home. It is OK, but I want to go to overnight camp with my brothers. My mother isn't going to allow that, until I am at least 11 years old.

Instead, during these summers, my parents and I and sometimes family friends, drive to Nippersink, a resort in Geneva City, Wisconsin. My parents and their friends have dinner together in the dining room. And their son Byron, who I did the Buster Brown modeling with.

During the day while at Nippersink, Byron and I do all different kinds of activities together. We canoe, or when it rains, watch movies. My favorite is *Blue Hawaii* with Elvis from 1965. We also swim, and play croquet, volleyball, tennis and more.

Meals are another fun part of the day. We walk from our hotel room across an enclosed bridge that seems to sway in the wind. Actually, Byron and I often run back and forth across the bridge, until we get caught by our parents and are told to stop running, because there are lots of people who use the bridge.

Byron has an older brother Peter, who is Miles' age. We sometimes get together as whole families, but mainly it's just Byron and me and our folks. Often on Sundays we order Kentucky Fried Chicken and bring it home to one of our houses for dinner. Those are the days no one talks about or knows how bad chicken skin is for you. We all enjoy the crispy chicken along with the skin.

*

Both our families had moved to the suburbs around the same time, and over the years we spent a lot of time together as families, though Byron and I don't go to the same school until we enter high school when all the neighborhood junior highs merge into one school.

One evening when Byron and I are in high school, we are at Bryon's house for a Sunday night dinner. He wants to know if I have a boyfriend or if I am dating anyone special. I do not want to share any of this information with him. It is none of his business. He is so nosy. We are in his room, waiting to go down for dinner, when he reaches over to me and gives me a kiss on the lips. I am in shock. We have been friends for as long as I can remember, and this really grosses me out. We are friends, I am not interested in him as a boyfriend. I don't even feel comfortable being friends with him after that.

9

Before we moved to the suburbs, my mother's cleaning lady Bertha told my mother she was very ill. She had cancer and would not be able to continue working for my mother. Sadly, Bertha passed away soon after, and her husband passed away a month later. I wonder if he died of a broken heart.

My mother interviewed more ladies to clean the house. She hired Susan, who came into my life when I was 4 years old. Susan has a heart of gold and I am so fortunate for her love and wisdom. I am sure she is in my life for a reason.

When we move to the new subdivision, Susan agrees to keep working for us. Susan takes the bus to the street near the entrance of our subdivision. She arrives at around 9:30 a.m.; unfortunately, I am already off to school. I am now in the second grade. I also take a bus, a school bus, and run home after school, especially to see Susan and get my bear hug. Even though Susan's bear hugs take my breath away, I love them anyway.

Susan and I have a very deep connection. She often reminds me that I am her daughter, and she is my mother. This is something we share only with each other and yet I always call her Susan not mom or mother. My mother sure does not make me feel the way Susan does—with love, kindness and respect for who I am, and Susan does not want to change me in anyway. Susan helps me grow into a positive mature person. I continue to call my mother, Mom, as it is true, but only biologically.

*

A couple of years after we move to the suburbs, two assassinations occur that rock Susan's world. The first one is on February 21, 1965, when Malcolm X is assassinated at a rally in New York City. Susan is so sad, and explains to me who Malcolm X was and how he was an advocate for Negroes in America. This is something my mother and father certainly did not teach me. They think I am too young to understand this type of brutal crime.

Then on April 4, 1968, Martin Luther King, Jr., is assassinated while standing on the balcony of the Lorraine Hotel in Memphis, Tennessee at 6:01 p.m. This is a very dark day for Susan, one of the darkest days I ever experience with her. I seldom see her cry. When she arrives on Friday April 5, she is distraught and crying, and I have never seen her like this, sad, withdrawn and angry.

I ask Susan what I can do to make her feel better. She walks over and gives me a hug. It isn't the usual bear hug. It is more of a one-arm hug with less spunk than usual. Susan suggests that I write a condolence card to Mrs. King, Coretta Scott King, Martin Luther King, Jr.'s widow. I do just that. And several weeks later, I can't believe it, but I receive a thank you note from Mrs. King, with her personal signature on her stationery.

I immediately call Susan at her home and tell her about the card I got in the mail that day from Mrs. King. She is so happy and tells me how proud she is of me, that I took the time to make such an important gesture. I write a report about it in fourth grade and am very proud. After all, Susan is my family, and I am Susan's family. I will do anything for Susan.

I am aware that Susan is also support and strength for my mother. My mother is a secretive person. Acting like things are always status quo, keeping her personality even-keeled most of the time, almost robotic. The only times I see other sides of her is when she is crying as a form of manipulation, or mad at her mother.

Around the same time, when I am still in fourth grade, I come home from school and want advice from my mother about my friends. Lynn and Mary and I are best friends but sometimes I feel left out.

That day I describe to my mother how Lynn and Mary have left me out during recess. They are whispering to each other and will not share with me what they are talking about. I am upset and ask my mother how to handle this in the future. She tells me that I am too giving to my friends. And if they are going to leave me out, I should look for new friends, because I should not give to friends unless I know I am going to receive something in return.

Even at 10 years old, I know something is very wrong with this statement. I thank my mother for her advice and go to my room to mull it over. I decide it isn't a good idea to discuss it further with her. I do not agree with her philosophy. Instead I know that giving to friends is not about what I will receive in return. And I know this because of the wonderful influence Susan has in my life. She often shares with me about her relationships with her friends at church, and how rewarding it is to give of oneself. NO question in my mind, having Susan as my "real mother" is a lifesaver.

10

When I am 11, my best friend since third grade, Lynn, and I convince my mother I am old enough to go to overnight camp. It is not an easy sell, especially since my mother is always in controlling, overprotective, smothering mode. After all, we only want to go to sleepover camp together, where my mother has gone, and my brother Warren is a camp tripper. A camp tripper is a counselor who takes campers on canoe trips.

She finally agrees, so, off to camp we go. Lynn and I request to be in the same cabin together. When we arrive at camp and find out we are not cabin mates, we both complain loudly to the counselors. For the sake of shutting us up, they make a couple of quick changes and we do end up in the same cabin together.

The cabin has room for twelve campers, six on each side of the cabin. When you walk into the cabin, the counselor has a room on the left side of the building. Across from her room on the right side of the cabin is the bathroom, which is pretty rustic, but at least we don't have to go outside of the cabin to use it. It has two showers, two toilet stalls and two sinks. Toward the back of the cabin are two sleeping sections on each side with bunk beds in them.

At night when one of us campers needs to use the bathroom, the strangest thing happens. At least it is strange at first, and then it is always very funny. When one of us is tinkling, those who are still awake start singing, "I Hear a Symphony," by Diana Ross and the Supremes. That first summer at camp, Carole King's album, *Tapestry*, has just come out and all of us sing, "I Feel the Earth Move Under My Feet" all day long, too.

Camp is fun, with many activities. Some of my favorites are arts and crafts, making tile things, trivets, wood letter holders that you can glue tiles on, lanyard necklaces and bracelets. We also make outrageous crème puffs, cut in half with vanilla ice cream inside and Saunders hot fudge on top.

I love to play baseball, swim and have relay races. Campfires are the best, with gooey marshmallows to make s'mores. It is fun to meet new kids and have dances with the boys' cabins. The boys are really cute.

The most fun for me is going on the canoe trips, which usually last two nights and three days. It is thrilling and I am always bragging about my brother Warren. He is the best canoe tripper and always makes us laugh. All the kids love him, especially the girls.

*

The second summer at camp is not as exciting as the first. This makes sense to me, as everything is familiar, not new and unknown like the first year. Lynn and I go together again. She is not very happy to be going this summer. She is the youngest of four children, and adolescence is taking its toll. Even though we bunk together, she becomes very homesick and goes home early. I do my best to enjoy the rest of the summer, make some new friends, and at least Warren is still a canoe tripper.

Halfway through camp, I start feeling funny. I have stomachaches and cramping. For the most part, I ignore it thinking it is something I ate that upset my stomach. This summer is when I get my first period. I go see the counselor and she is very helpful and sets me up with the supplies I need. Fortunately, I am aware that this will occur; we learn about puberty and sex education in 5th grade.

*

The third summer, I go to camp with my friend Mary. Mary is my first friend when I move to the suburbs. We move into our new houses at the same time, in late summer, and meet while trick or treating. But Mary is a wimp. Or maybe it is me that is a wimp that summer. We arrive at camp together and we both have bunks on the left side of the cabin. We unpack and settle in.

Warren is not at camp this summer and I am instantly homesick, missing that protection and comfort zone that he is for me. I am unhappy and not willing to give camp a chance this summer. I stay for about five days and then take the easy way out and say I want to go home. I figure if Lynn did it last summer, I can too.

My parents pick me up and bring me home. I am happy to leave camp behind and do not plan on going back again. My mother seems to understand, which is surprising. My Uncle Simon stops by for a visit that same afternoon and I find it very embarrassing in front of him. He makes me feel like a quitter.

11

And now the nightmare begins…

The symptoms start when I am just 13. I get my period that summer at overnight camp. It is late summer, and I am back at school in eighth grade. I am having trouble getting out of bed in the morning. I tell my mother I don't feel well and want to stay home from school. This works on several different occasions. But she starts catching on and realizes I am not sick. Not sick like having a temperature, cold or flu; I just don't have any desire to forge ahead into the day.

I know I am unhappy. I guess I might say I am going into a depression. I feel down and lethargic, not wanting to participate in life. I am just too afraid to say the word "depression" out loud. *My maternal grandmother had been administered shock treatments many times for her depression, and I didn't want to associate myself with this.* If I admit to my mother I am feeling down, who knows what she will do next? Will I have to see Dr. Turner? He scares me. I met him a couple of times when I was with my mother and my grandmother for visits with him. He is very tall, wears glasses, and smokes a pipe and never smiles. And the tobacco does not smell good.

After fighting with my mother once again about staying home from school, I realize that this particular day I have no chance of winning. She insists that I get my clothes on, eat breakfast and make the bus on time. I get my clothes on and come to breakfast in jeans and a smock top. The smock top buttons up the front with a floral pattern, with small sleeves that look like ruffles on my shoulders. My mother is very unhappy with me and asks me why I have to wear that top again. I have been wearing it for days on end and she doesn't understand why I don't wear something different. I know why. I don't care about what I am wearing, I can't decide what to wear, and I just wear the same thing over and over again.

For some reason, this is the end of the rope for my mom. That day when I get home from school, my mother tells me she is taking me to see my pediatrician. She immediately drives me to Dr. Smith's office. He examines me and I answer a lot of questions. My mother is in the room, which makes me very uncomfortable, so answering them is difficult. I don't want to say the wrong thing and disappoint her, and I am not sure how much to reveal to the doctor about how I am really feeling. He decides it will be a good idea for me to take antidepressants.

I am now out of the closet. Once Dr. Smith gives me the prescription for antidepressants my mother knows and acknowledges that I am in a depression. (I am not on lithium yet.)

I do not want to take any pills. How will they make me feel better? Will they really work? I have to take them three times a day, which means I have to take one during school. My mother puts the pill in a baggy in my lunch; it is so embarrassing. I am in eighth grade and it is a small lunchroom and everyone will see me taking the pill.

But my mother has the perfect solution. Let's lie and tell everyone that the pill is for my allergies. I don't have any allergies. So that is what I end up doing, lying, telling my friends that the little blue pill that looks like a miniature football is for my allergies. It is uncomfortable for me to lie; however, my mother has no problem lying in order to manipulate and work her agenda.

The depression continues and I am not able to skip school anymore. That is over. But I often wear the same thing to school. And I am not sure why some of my friends put up with me and still sit with me on the bus and have lunch with me. I always go straight home after school. I don't go to friends' houses anymore, and at this point they don't ask me over either. Who can blame them? I am not any fun to be around. I even hate my own company.

12

During the fall I am riding my bike in the neighborhood and a mom is taking her son for a ride on his tricycle. She asks me how old I am and if I will babysit for her son. I tell her I am 13 and would love to babysit for her son. I give her my phone number and she calls my mother to find out more about my experience with children. She sets up a date for me to come to her house to meet and get to know her son James.

Mrs. Mullins is pregnant with her second child and due in the early spring. She asks me to babysit for James every Saturday night and be a mother's helper and assist her during the summer with the baby she is expecting. This works out well for me considering I am not going back to overnight camp and will need something to do this summer.

James is a cute little boy. He is 3 when I start babysitting for him. He loves for me to read him countless books at bedtime. Mrs. Mullins kids me about that. She says I spoil him, and they have to read countless books to him at bedtime as well.

After reading all the books to James, he falls asleep quickly. I go down to the kitchen and find a snack for myself. Mrs. Mullins is always on some kind of a diet and does not have yummy snacks, so sometimes I bring snacks from home.

*

Carol is the name Mr. and Mrs. Mullins give their daughter. She is a premature baby, born four weeks early. Carol is in an incubator and has to remain at the hospital for a month before she can come home to her new family.

When Carol comes home from the hospital with her parents, she is very tiny, weighing just over five pounds. At first I notice that Mr. Mullins carries her into the house. He asks me to hold her. It is now over one month since Mrs. Mullins had her baby and she is back on her feet feeling well.

While I am holding Carol, Mrs. Mullins sits down with me. She wants to discuss the hours I will be helping her with Carol. It turns out she wants me to be at her house Monday through Friday every week during the summer from 8:30 a.m. to 5:00 p.m. These are the same hours Mr. Mullins is at his office. He is an attorney.

At first I am not sure I want to spend so much of my summer as a mother's helper. Mrs. Mullins is very convincing. She insists she needs the help, and it is hard for me to say no. I am happy about all the money I will be making that summer.

Mr. Mullins is the one who teaches me how to take care of Carol. He shows me how to change her diaper, warm up her bottle, feed her and bathe her. Mrs. Mullins is a bystander.

I tell my mother how Mrs. Mullins depends on me to take care of Carol the whole day while Mr. Mullins is at work. And during the summer, I do not see Mrs. Mullins pick up or hold Carol. Mrs. Mullins will often tell me she is tired and goes to her bedroom to rest.

When fall comes along and summer is over, it is back to school for me. I still babysit James and Carol on Saturday nights, and Mrs. Mullins asks me to come over after school for a couple of hours three days a week.

*

I keep a babysitting log. I also have a steady babysitting job for the neighbors who live on the corner. They have two kids, Julie and Robert. They are on a bowling team every Sunday, and I walk to their house at dinner time and get a ride home when it is dark out.

The result of the babysitting log is that I put half the money in my savings account to buy a car when I am 16 or 17. I record the date, who I babysit for, the number of hours, and the amount of money I make. The money accumulates quickly.

13

I am in eighth grade when I have my first boyfriend. He looks like Robert Redford. His name is Peter and he lives twenty minutes away by car. He often comes to my house on his Solex, which is a bike with a motor. My friend Nancy and Peter are neighbors. She introduces me to Peter. She has a crush on him; she isn't very happy that he likes me.

Peter's father is a record manager and producer on the side, an electrician as his day job. Peter invites me to go to a private concert. He tells me that Eddie Kendrick, the lead singer of the Temptations is going to sing, and Anne Murray is going to sing as well.

We arrive at the concert hall and I am awestruck by how beautiful a building it is. The interior is like a museum. Everywhere you look there is another beautiful sight, with high ceilings, decorative moldings and artwork. Peter's dad takes us right to the front row of the theatre. There are about thirty people already in their seats behind us.

The deep red velvet curtain opens and there is Anne Murray sitting on a stool, with a microphone in her hand. She sings one of her hits, "Snowbird." I am having a hard time listening closely, waiting for Eddie Kendrick to come on next. He is one of my favorites.

Anne Murray finishes singing, and we all clap. She walks off the stage and Eddie walks on. He is so tall and thin and has a burgundy suit that matches the velvet curtain. It fits him like a glove. He has a goatee and mustache; he is so handsome. Eddie begins to sing; "Keep on Truckin'," "Boogie Down," "If You Let Me" and many more.

This is just the beginning of the concerts I attend. Seeing Eddie Kendrick perform is the only small concert I go to. Other larger venues were Smokey Robinson, Marvin Gay, Deep Purple, The Beach Boys, Peter Frampton, Chicago, The Doobie Brothers, Jethro

Tull, America, Eagles, Bette Midler and the Supremes. Going to concerts is the best time of my teenage years.

One night I take Peter to a party at my friend Mary's house. It is a making out party and that's what all the kids are doing. We are all in eighth grade, but Peter is in ninth grade, meaning we are still in junior high and Peter is already in high school. He is moving a little too fast for me and wants more than kissing. I don't, so that is the last time I go to a party with Peter.

Nancy is very happy. After I tell her how the party went, she grabs him, and they date for a couple of years.

*

When I enter high school, the ninth grade is daunting. There are so many older kids and many different clicks. There are the cheerleaders and jocks, the rich kids, the greasers and so on. My depression has not gone away. At this point different symptoms are occurring. I am having a great deal of pain in my neck.

Seriously, when you look at my face straight on you can see that my neck must hurt. It is so swollen that my neck looks like it is disappearing. It looks like my head is on my shoulders. People say I look like a pro football player. Once again, my mother takes me to my pediatrician's office. After examining me, he tells my mother that I need to see a specialist. He thinks I am having a problem with my thyroid and it is out of his area of expertise.

Off we go to see the thyroid specialist, an endocrinologist, Dr. Young. He is a short man, with a round face and glasses. He speaks very slowly. He tells my mother and me that I will need extensive testing, and the first part of the testing will be blood work. He gives my mother a prescription for the blood work and tells us we need to go to a hospital to get the blood drawn.

My mother has been a volunteer at the local hospital for over twenty years. She volunteers every other Thursday and wears this salmon jumper over her clothes. Her job is to take patients in wheelchairs to the x-ray department. She waits for them to have their x-ray and takes them back to their rooms. Since Dr. Young did not specify which hospital to go to for the blood work, she takes me where she is most familiar, where she volunteers.

When we get there, we go straight to the laboratory where I will have my blood drawn. This is a first for me. We sit in the waiting area until they call me. Needless to say, my mother comes right along. I am 15, and I would rather go myself. It ends up it is a good thing I don't.

The assistant tells me to sit down in this chair that has a half tray that I need to rest my arm on. The phlebotomist, the person who draws blood, walks over to me and takes my left arm and puts it on the tray. She then takes a tourniquet, which resembles a long wide rubber band, and ties it around my left arm, above my elbow, where my muscle is. She proceeds to clean the inside of my elbow with alcohol. She feels around for a vein, and after she seems to find one, she inserts the needle, and nothing happens. She moves the needle around inside my arm a couple of times. It hurts, but still nothing happens. She then says, "I am new at this. I need to go get some help," and she walks away leaving the needle in my arm. My mother speaks up and quickly another phlebotomist sees what is happening and runs over to help.

The new phlebotomist removes the needle from my left arm and tells me to keep my arm up in the air. She takes my right arm and goes through the whole process again. This time the phlebotomist with more experience gets my blood on the first try. She warns us that I may have a bruise on my left arm, but not to worry, it will heal.

Later that day, I show my mother my left arm. It doesn't look like my arm. Instead it has a large egg-like bump, and a bruise is starting to appear around the bump. My mother dismisses my worry and says it will heal.

The next morning, my arm is much worse. It looks like someone beat me. Once again, we are off to Dr. Smith's office. He takes one look at my arm and tells us it is a hematoma. That the blood is stuck in my arm, which has caused the large bump and bruises. He says it will take several weeks for the bruises to heal, and that I may have pain in the area for a while after the bruises are gone.

He is right, it takes a long time to heal and I have pain in the elbow area for months. When it is time to have my blood drawn again, which is often, they are not able to use my left arm. I have nightmares about the phlebotomist leaving the needle in my arm.

(Again, many years later, I will learn how bad a decision this was to inject me with iodine.) The technician injects iodine into the vein in my arm, and then I have to wait for at least an hour before the iodine is in my bloodstream. The tech then takes the nuclear test.

After Dr. Young gets the results from the first scan, he tells me that I have Hashimoto's thyroiditis, rare in someone my age. Since the hospital is a teaching hospital, Dr. Young is eager to have all the interns and residents look at my test results and feel my neck. I feel like a caged animal in the zoo.

The residents at this teaching hospital love to feel my neck and thyroid and view all the x-rays and scans, because for someone who has Hashimoto's thyroiditis, the thyroid is a different shape.

Dr. Young thinks it will be a good idea to prescribe steroids to reduce the inflammation in my neck area. No one is asking my opinion; why would they? I start on the steroid pack, with the dosage being larger at first and then weaning over time. The steroids work in that they reduce the swelling; however, there are two side effects. One is a twenty-five-pound weight gain, and the other one is that my depression gets worse.

When I go off the steroids, I lose the twenty-five pounds, but my neck area becomes swollen again. Dr. Young thinks it is a good idea to keep repeating this process of on and off steroids. For a year, I go through the same thing over and over. At 16 I even have the stretch marks to prove it.

*

Dr. Young finally gets fed up with my mother and by default, me too. I think Dr. Young does not want to deal with my mother repeatedly calling him with demands to fix me. He gives up on being my doctor and tells my mother that he can't help me, and that I have some type of psychiatric disorder. And the best place for me will be the psychiatric unit. I break out in a sweat, as I know too much about psychiatric units, this can't be happening. He knows about my grandmother's history of depression and uses that as an excuse to say I have a psychiatric disorder.

My mother does not call my father after Dr. Young says I need to go into the psychiatric unit. She does not call or contact anyone. She just lets the nurse take me over to the psych unit and finally she is rid of me. I am sure she will be celebrating tonight.

*

They wheel me into the psychiatric unit immediately after seeing Dr. Young. It has locks on the outside of the door. I get this strange feeling that my life is over, I have no control, no one sees me. I am lost and no one understands what is happening to me, especially me. It is terrifying.

The nurse wheels me into a hospital room and tells me that I will not be able to have any visitors for a few days, until I settle into being in this new unit, the psychiatric unit. I will have a new doctor. His name is Dr. Harris, and he is a psychiatrist. Now I am really afraid, petrified.

*

I remember that my grandmother used to see Dr. Turner and she would go into the hospital and have shock treatments for her depression. She had left Europe when she was 19 to come to America. At the time, my grandfather was already here, and he sent for her and her sister. Soon after, World War I broke out and my grandmother's family perished in their European villages. My grandmother had to live her whole life carrying the survival guilt that she got out before her family perished. I can't even imagine how horrible that was for her.

*

Soon after I had stopped seeing Peter, I met Peter's friend, Jim, who goes to my high school. Jim has a husky build, curly brown hair and a great smile. We like each other a lot and spend time together going to movies and out to dinner. I especially enjoy going out to dinner with Jim's family on Sundays to my favorite Italian restaurant. Jim is the oldest of three boys and his mother loves having another female along for the ride and dinner. Jim and Peter's fathers are in business together.

Jim often showers me with gifts. For my Sweet Sixteen, he gives me a heart-shaped amethyst necklace with baby pearls set all around the heart; it is so pretty.

*

Jim and I are dating when Dr. Young tells my mother she has to sign me into the psychiatric ward at the hospital. Jim knows I am going to the hospital that day for testing and comes to see me in my regular hospital room. He can't find me there, so he asks at the nurses' station where I am. Have I gone home? They tell him there has been a transfer to another floor by the doctor. They tell Jim it is the east wing and that he may not be able to visit me there. There are no HIPPA laws at this time, prohibiting the medical staff from revealing any information about the patient. So the nurses freely give away this information.

Jim is going to find me. He brings a dozen yellow roses and comes to the east wing to give them to me. He knocks on the door and I just happen to be walking nearby. There are two long windows, floor to ceiling on either side of the door, which has a lock on the outside of it. It is the kind of glass that has wires running through it, so in case someone tries to break it, it will not shatter everywhere.

Jim finds it surprising that he cannot open the door. He tugs and pulls at it and makes all sorts of noise. The psych nurse goes up to the window and tells Jim that only immediate family can visit me. And since he isn't that, he has to leave immediately or she will call security for the disturbance he is causing. The nurse decides to unlock the door to take the yellow roses from Jim to give to me. They are gorgeous and fragrant.

*

In the psych ward, I am watching people being taken away on gurneys, for that same shock treatment that my grandmother got. They come back sometime later that day, and they seem out of it. I am sure I am going to be next.

For now, I will go to the common room, the room where patients have meals and watch TV or read books. I wait there for my doctor to come and see me. I wait day after day, for what seems like forever. I ask the nurse every day when my doctor will be coming, and she never has a clear answer.

Finally, after being in the psychiatric unit for a week, Dr. Harris shows up. He takes me into a room that has a couple of chairs in it. We both sit down, and he introduces himself to me and begins to apologize for not seeing me for the first week I am in the unit. He tries to explain by telling me that he has had a family event with many out-of-town guests.

After we speak for a while, he tells me that he thinks I am manic depressive, and he wants to have me start taking medication, lithium. I ask him what all this means, and he tells me it will help with my mood swings. I really am not sure what that means, but I do understand that changes in my mood are often going on when I am on steroids.

After that first meeting, he sees me every day for another week and then tells me I am ready to go home, but will have to stay on the lithium to control my mood swings. My parents pick me up from the hospital, and life as I know it will never be the same.

*

Two weeks is a very long time to be in the hospital without being able to see Jim. He thinks so too. And after discussing my situation with his mother, he is forbidden to communicate with me. Not that I understand why I am in the psych ward in the first place. Jim is close to his mother and I understand that, even then.

She wants to protect him, and once she finds out I am "manic depressive," it is time for Jim to find another girlfriend. It takes me a while to get over him.

Unfortunately, I am busy with many other things going on in my life. I am furious at my parents. My mother never thinks of the consequences of her decisions and my father is not a part of the decision-making. I do get over Jim, but I really miss him, his mom and those Sunday night dinners. I am always searching for a mother figure, often without even realizing it.

*

Returning to high school after two weeks in the psych ward is very hard to do. All the kids stare at me all the time. There is an open area between parts of the building that has benches. I sometimes sit there between classes and try to fade into the woodwork. I am not successful at it; everyone still stares. Scarves are in fashion and that works out well for me. I wear a scarf around my neck and the whispering and gossip continue about me and my thyroid surgery. Kids are so mean they make up whatever stories they want.

14

My mother takes me to see Dr. Harris once a week. She sits in the waiting room while I see the doctor. He is a short man with a pleasant face and a full beard. I notice that his pants are always short on him. That bothers me. I'm not sure why, but it does. He always talks to me about the same thing, asking me why I am anxious. I don't know. I never have a clear answer for him. The visits make me uncomfortable, and I feel like it is a waste of time.

I do have Dr. Harris on my side when I ask him if I can go to Europe with a group of kids from my school. He thinks it is a good idea. My mother hates the idea, but somehow feels she has to listen to what he recommends. Dr Harris feels that it will be good for me to be away from my family and surroundings for a while and spend time with children my age.

*

When I get out of the hospital, in addition to seeing Dr. Harris, we need to find a new endocrinologist, since we definitely will not be seeing Dr. Young again. I begin seeing Dr. Howard, who orders Synthroid for me, which is a thyroid replacement medication. He does extensive blood work and what seems like countless thyroid scans. He determines that I have Hashimoto's thyroiditis, which I already know. Hashimoto's is rare; one in a million have it. Having it at 14–15 years of age is unusual as well. Besides my thyroid being a different shape, it is hyperthyroid that burns out to hypothyroid, which means I need replacement therapy to keep my goiter/neck from becoming swollen.

If only I would have seen Dr. Howard first, I may never have been put on steroids, which did not work, and might never have been thrown in a psych ward, and I may have never been put on lithium.

15

For years, my mother has an arrangement with my grandmother. My mother calls my grandmother every day at 9 a.m. and 5 p.m. Just to check in. I think this is the plan Monday through Friday, and the weekends are different, because my mom and I visit my grandmother every Saturday afternoon, and each Sunday my grandmother has dinner with one of her four children that live locally.

My mother resents having to check in at these times. I am not around at 9 a.m., but I am usually home at 5 p.m. My mother always looks at the clock around 5 p.m. and complains that she has to call her mother. When she forgets to call, my grandmother calls my mother at 5:01 p.m. or 5:02 p.m. and says, "Sally, what's wrong; why don't you call me on time?"

While on the phone, my mother sits at the desk in the kitchen, which is a piece of white Formica with gold flicks in it, next to the refrigerator, with a cabinet with two doors on the wall above the desk, and three drawers on the base of the Formica. She places one of the six kitchen chairs at the desk and sits with the first drawer of the desk open, where she has the paper clips in a tuna can that has contact paper around it. My mother plays with the paper clips. Just as she does when she is doing her shopping on the phone.

She just complains to my grandmother that she has a lot going on during that time of day and sometimes it slips her mind to call her. My mother then often hangs up the phone quite abruptly. She looks at me and tells me that she promises, yes promises, never to do this to me when I am older and on my own. She is good at breaking promises.

*

When Susan arrives at our house three times a week, my mother has a fresh pot of coffee waiting for her. Susan comes in and sits down at the kitchen table and has her coffee, and my mother talks to her about whatever it is that she keeps to herself, meaning not speaking to any of her friends or relatives about the topics that she shares with Susan, especially looking for advice and audience from Susan, as if Susan is her therapist. God only knows how many times I beg my mother to see a therapist. She actually went once and then says that she doesn't need a therapist, code words for "I have Susan for that, and I think I am fine."

Susan always teaches me that in order to fix a problem, no matter what kind, you need to identify it, recognize that it is a problem. That is the first step. Then the second step is to make changes in your life to eliminate the problem. This sounds logical to me. Be honest with yourself and find peace in knowing that you are going to become a better person by making positive changes to enrich your life and keep growing.

Denial is my mother's middle name. If she can find a way to put an issue on the back burner, she will. She will leave it there until Susan comes to be her ear, to listen and guide her. I think my mother lives in the closet about many things, especially things having to do with me.

When it comes to my mental well-being, the closet is full of secrets. It is no surprise that she will invent lies about my mental health and what my diagnosis is. I will sometimes hear her talking to her brothers and sisters-in-law, as well as some of my older cousins, about me. (I am the youngest of all the cousins on my mother's side of the family.) I have trouble following the stories she tells and excuses she makes about me and some of my behavior, and how she often exaggerates my behavior.

16

My parents want to keep me busy and summer is around the corner. My mother suggests I get a job. That actually sounds good to me. Getting out of my house and away from my parents, especially my mother, will be the best and healthiest thing for me.

My mom and I each scour the local want ads and come up with an ad looking for an assistant at a CPA's office for the summer. I call and they ask me to come in for an interview. I am 15 and do not have a driver's license yet, so my mother drives me to the interview. The CPA's office is 15 minutes from home. It looks more like a house that is now an office.

There are three desks side by side in a basement, and that is where the interview takes place. I get the job. My duties are to balance a ledger card system for the CPA's billing system. Math has always been my strength; the learning curve is a small one. The hours are 8:30 to 4:00, Monday through Friday.

My mother drives me there every day and picks me up as well. I think this is nice of her, but it does get me out of her hair. I bring a brown bag lunch every day and eat at my desk. My boss loves that; more productivity out of me. I make over $200 a week, which is a lot of money at 15 years old.

Over time the job becomes tedious and boring, so the following spring, I call a larger CPA firm and see about a different job for the coming summer. It turns out the son of the owner of this CPA firm, which by the way is in a real office building in an office park, is a couple years older than me and we go to the same high school.

I approach Mr. Sommer, and he is very open to having extra help during the summer months. I get the job. The office is beautiful, with high ceilings and enormous glass windows from floor to ceiling, along with many tall plants in beautiful large ceramic pots. They have a plant service that comes every week to care for and water the plants. I am responsible for reconciling the time sheets for all the CPAs and making sure the billing goes out correctly to the clients.

17

That summer I am 16 and am learning how to drive and will soon be able to relieve my mother from her job of driving me to and from work. I take a driver's class through "Easy Method Driving School." The instructor isn't the most patient person. He teaches me how to parallel park for the first time. And believe it or not, I do it correctly. So that is the only time he has me parallel park, not really enough times to be good at it. Otherwise the class is uneventful.

I pass the driving test, and now that I have my license, I am able to use my brother Lee's white Monte Carlo to go to school and to my part-time job after school. The reason Lee's car is available to me is because he drives over to our house first thing in the morning around 7:30 a.m. and parks his car in our driveway. My dad and he drive to the hardware store together for the day.

It works out pretty well for my junior year in high school. When I am 17 going into my senior year in high school, I buy a car of my own. I am able to do that with the money I have in my savings account from my summer jobs and gift money from my parents and grandparents.

My grandmother Francine, my mother's mother, gives all four of us kids one thousand dollars as a gift toward our cars when we purchase them. I also take an interest-free loan from my parents for a thousand dollars, which I pay back over ten months, one hundred dollars a month.

I buy a used 1973 Gran Torino. It is hunter green with a white pinstripe on each side, lots of extras and leather seats as well. It is the same car that Starsky and Hutch drive in their television show, but theirs is fire engine red with the cool white racing stripes on the sides. You know, growing up in the Midwest with four men in the house, I am pretty up on cars. I am not sure about the Gran Torino right away. Since the previous owner keeps it in the garage all the time and it has very low mileage I decide to buy it. I pay $3300 for it.

I am proud of my new car. At least it is new to me. The majority of my friends get new cars that year as well; they all get Chevy Chevettes. Two years after buying my Gran Torino, I trade it in for a Grand Prix. It is a demo. They often have low mileage and you can get a great deal on them.

My Grand Prix is a beauty. It is a great looking car and it also has loads of extras. It is dark burgundy with a burgundy hard top, which is hard leather that covers the back part of the roof of the car. While I am driving my new, well almost new, 1978 Grand Prix, all my friends are still driving their Chevettes.

My friends and I love to go to the Howard Johnson near the highway together. They often ask me to drive because everyone loves my car. Lynn, Chris and Mary and I go for dessert to HoJos. We order five different scoops of ice cream that come in an incredibly large glass ice cream dish that is on a pedestal.

*

One of the highlights of my senior year is that I am in a co-op program, another way to escape interacting with my classmates. I get credit for the last two course hours of my day at high school if I have a job. At the time, I have no medical background whatsoever. The school asks me if I want to work at a cardiologist's office, working as a receptionist, along with other front desk duties. The medical office is about five minutes away from the school. I think it is a great opportunity. Hank Coffer, MD, is a cardiologist and will be my new boss. Let me clarify that, *Mrs.* Coffer is going to be my boss.

I report for work at 1:30 p.m. to 5:30 p.m., Monday through Friday. Mrs. Coffer introduces me to Judy, the office manager, who trains me. Learning how to answer the phone and make appointments is a breeze. Filing isn't a joy, but necessary none the less. The time does fly by and I enjoy the office environment.

After a few weeks at my new co-op position, Mrs. Coffer takes me aside and tells me she sees great potential in me, and that my skills are a waste at the front desk. They can teach me how to do EKGs and assist with stress testing and mount and stick the results on special paper for Dr. Coffer. I am a bit apprehensive, not being familiar with these tests. Mrs. Coffer puts me at ease and tells me that I will have plenty of support.

Peggy, Dr. Coffer's assistant, takes me under her wing and trains me. First the EKGs. It is 1976 and with these EKG machines, it is difficult to attach the leads to the patients. The first patient that I am going to do an EKG on has special circumstances; because of her breast implants, As my eyes open larger, I start to feel uncomfortable. Peggy assures me that I do the EKG the same way on all patients. The only difference is that when the patient is lying down, her breasts will not be. They remain the same as if she is sitting or standing up.

Every day I do at least three or four EKGs. Mrs. Coffer thinks that I am ready to assist with stress tests. Dr. Coffer performs the stress tests Monday through Friday with Peggy assisting. He has another cardiologist, Dr. Nadu, who comes in on Saturdays to perform more stress tests. Mrs. Coffer and Peggy feel that I am more than ready to assist during the test. The training is straightforward. The patient first stands by a treadmill while the leads are put on their chest. A blood pressure cuff is put on the patient's left arm. The patient then steps onto the treadmill and begins walking slowly.

Over time we increase the speed of the treadmill and the doctor monitors the patient's heart rate and blood pressure. This particular patient is a gentleman in his early fifties who needs to take the stress test to renew his pilot's license. Dr. Nadu is watching his progress.

During my training, I find out that once the patient gets to 90% of their heart rate, the test is over and the patient gets off the treadmill. A calculation is done prior to the patient beginning the test. In this case I am also observing the monitor and watching the current rates. I see that the patient is at 87% and ask Dr. Nadu if we can start slowing the speed of the treadmill. He says no. At 91% I ask Dr. Nadu if I can stop the test. He insists it is fine to push the patient past his 90%.

Within minutes the patient collapses and falls off the treadmill. I do not wait for any instructions from Dr. Nadu. Instead, I run to the nearest telephone and call 9-1-1. They arrive within five minutes and take the patient to the hospital. He has had a heart attack and will not be able to renew his pilot's license. Because Dr. Nadu did not follow protocol the patient will suffer. And I certainly have a mistrust of all doctors going forward.

18

And now we've come full circle to where this book began…and the story continues.

After the trip to Indiana, and the events around my first lithium toxicity when I was 17, and after the four days in seclusion in the psychiatric hospital, you may recall that Dr. Snyder decided it would be best to admit me to a psychiatric hospital, Woodridge, for a while. I did not have any choice in the matter. He insisted it would help me get back on my feet.

As it turns out my parents are in on it. They have to attend my father's biannual hardware show in Chicago. I'm not sure if Susan is not available or if my parents just don't want to spend the money for her to stay with me. So instead they cut a deal with the shrink. If he can keep me in the psych hospital for two to three extra days more than he plans, they can use the hospital as a babysitter for me. Dr. Snyder says our health insurance will pay for the few extra days, so, "No problem."

I certainly am old enough, and intuitive enough to see what is going on here. What are my parents thinking? How can they leave me in a psychiatric hospital for even one extra minute than necessary? They have me in the closet, God forbid that anyone even knows where I am. They might have to explain that their daughter is manic depressive; they don't ever want to do that.

During that hospital stay, I get in trouble one night. Every hospital room has two patients in it. When I check into the psychiatric hospital, the room I am in does not have another patient in it. I feel fortunate not to have to deal with a roommate. But that does not last long.

I meet Sherry in the common room and we become friendly. Sherry is a couple years older than me and is in the hospital for drug addiction. Funny, one of the reasons I am there is because the doctor prescribes too *much* medication.

After I am there a couple of days, an elderly woman comes in to share my room with me. She is really out of it, and scary too. She is short and her clothes are big and baggy on her. Her gray hair is a mess, and she talks to herself.

The patient rooms have a connecting door, similar to a hotel. The connecting door leads into the next patient room, which also has two beds in it. Sherry sees how upset I am about my new roommate. She suggests that I move my twin bed through the connecting door into her room. She will push the two beds together that are already in her room to make room for my bed.

When we finish the move, the nurse walks into Sherry's room. She demands to know what is going on and what did we think we are doing? Remodeling the hospital rooms? I tell her that I am afraid to stay with my new roommate. She doesn't care, and orders me to move the bed back and to meet her at the end of the hall.

"The end of the hall." I am not sure what that means but something in my gut tells me it isn't going to be good. Once I return the bed to my hospital room, I walk to the end of the hallway with Sherry.

The nurse takes me by the forearm and tells me I have to go into seclusion. I have NO idea what she is talking about. Needless to say, I find out very quickly exactly what she means by seclusion. She pushes me into the room that has only one doorway. It has a bare mattress on the floor and a window to the outside that you cannot see out of, unless you are seven feet tall. There is one small window in the door that has metal running through the glass.

She tells me that I am misbehaving, and I have to remain in seclusion until she feels that I am calm. She closes the door and locks it. I sit down on the floor, not wanting to go anywhere near the mattress. I do not have a watch on, because when you sign into one of these looney bins, you have to surrender all your personal things, even shoelaces and belts.

Time stands still. I stare at the ceiling for a while and try to understand how my life has come to this. Then I close my eyes and imagine my favorite things, like eating jelly thumbprints cookies at my Grandmother Paula's house and doing jigsaw puzzles with my dad, working on my needlepoints and listening to music.

I am in seclusion for almost two hours according to Sherry, since I do not have an opportunity to look at the clock before being put in seclusion. Sherry is crying while waiting on the floor by the locked door for me.

This is just another event that increases my claustrophobia. In everyday life I do not notice it, except when on an elevator or in a room without any windows. We are not born claustrophobic; it is these negative experiences that end up being life altering.

When they pick me up from the psychiatric hospital after the hardware show, I tell them that I met this really cute guy at group therapy. And that he wants to visit me at our house, and I have already given him our address and phone number and he is planning on visiting soon, as we are both going home today. He did visit me once. He looks like John Travolta. They are not too happy about having him over; serves them right.

19

It is now my senior year and I have been missing many days of school. I've lost track of how many days. My mother convinces Dr. Snyder to once again admit me to the psych ward, this time just because she feels like it. My grandmother is bothering her more and she wants her space, so why not admit me to the psych ward, while she can still do it legally? I am not 18 yet. What a monster. I feel like running away from home, but where am I going to go?

Many of my teachers understand why I am not at school. I can only imagine what lies my mother must be feeding them, except for one English teacher, Mr. Canary. He does not want to hear any of it; doctors' letters do not sway him. The only way I am going to be able to graduate from high school is to write four extra papers for him. I have all A's in my other courses, and if I don't produce the papers, I will fail his course. I write the papers.

I go to my Senior Prom with a guy I meet while working for a doctor. He is an accountant. His name is Stuart and he is a really nice guy, tall, over six feet, a dark complexion and a great smile. He is at least four years older than I am and does not know anyone in my high school class. I am too weird for anyone from my class to ask me to go to the prom. I am lucky to have met Stuart.

Graduation day comes and I am able to participate. Over 500 hundred of us have our white robes on with graduation caps that have a red and white tousle and a piece of metal that has "76" on it. The graduation takes place on the football field. The principal announces our names as we walk up the five or six steps to the stage where the podium is. He shakes our hand and hands a mock certificate of graduation to each and every one of us. We then walk down the steps at the other end of the stage. That is it, over in two minutes. I can't believe it is so short with all the time we spent in high school. And with me missing a lot of it because of illness and hospitalizations it feels like it should be more significant.

20

Stacey moves into town our senior year of high school. Lucky for me she needs a friend and does not believe all the rumors about me. Missing all that school, several different stories are going around the school about me. She lives with her family in a Victorian-looking apartment about two or three miles from my house. We often go home after school together on the school bus directly to her apartment.

Stacey's mother has passed away, and her father wants to live closer to his older children from a previous marriage, so he moves Stacey and her older brother John from Chicago to Michigan to be near their older siblings. From hanging out at Stacey's apartment I get to know John. He is a really nice guy, tall and in great shape. Not the best-looking person, but his personality and charm make up for it. He asks me out and we start dating.

I worry about how it will affect my friendship with Stacey. I didn't have too much to worry about there. John and I decide we are better as friends. So he introduces me to his best friend Jack. He and Jack go to the local university a few towns north. I am attending the same university at the time. Soon Jack and I start dating and it gets very serious very quickly.

While attending the university I live at home. I have a part-time job, approximately twenty-five hours a week working in a medical office, for my friend's father, Dr. Reese. I share the responsibility of posting Blue Cross Blue Shield explanation of benefits. Brenda and I share this job. She has been working for the group for several years. Brenda is relatively lazy, but good at posting. She comes to work and sits at her desk and only gets up to go to lunch or use the restroom. Like my mother, her body type is pear in shape, with wide hips; I think it is from sitting too much. "Secretary spread" is one term for that.

Dr. Reese hires me because of my experience working for CPAs and other medical practices. He feels I have the right skills to get the job done. Brenda is never completely caught up with the posting, which in turn causes the billing to be late every month. In order to send statements to the patients on time, all insurance payments need to be recorded first. At this time there are few computers for billing purposes in doctors' private practices. All the posting has to be done manually, by hand, on a pegboard system.

Overall, it is a well-run office. The four physicians are internists, and no one asks me to assist with the patients. Martin Salem, MD, is one of the physicians in the practice. He has a wonderful sense of humor. He can make anyone laugh and he knows that he can.

*

Jack comes from a family of three boys. He is the youngest. His father is a UPS driver, and his mother works at a woman's clothing store. His oldest brother Larry and wife Jean have two small boys, and Larry works for Sears Tire and lives nearby. Jack's middle brother Mark and wife Molly live an hour north of town and Mark works for a railroad company.

Ellen, Jack's mother, and I have a rocky relationship at best, which seems unusual for me. I get along with most people. I try many things to find a way into her heart; loving her son doesn't seem to be reason enough for her to like me. She is not a warm and fuzzy person. She stands about 5' 2", is stocky, wears glasses and has beady eyes. No one is good enough for her sons and she makes that very clear.

Eventually all three of her sons get divorces at her hand. Jack's father is a little more affectionate, but is a little scary too. He is about 5' 10" with a bulky build, wears glasses, and his face has lots of wrinkles. His wrinkles are the scary part; possibly too much exposure to the elements being a UPS driver.

After local university, Jack and I attend our state university together. I am living in a dorm and he lives in an apartment with two friends. While at university, my major is interior design, with minors in art history and business. Jack is taking accounting and business.

His mother really hates that we are away from home studying at the same university. She openly objects to our spending time alone together. Strangely, even though I am not her choice for her baby son, she wants us to marry. Do the right thing in her mind.

*

When we have been dating almost two years, I become ill. I am 19. That is, I start having a reaction to the lithium. Especially after the lithium toxicity I went through when I was 17, I certainly am familiar with the symptoms.

Because of this I am able to contact my doctor and tell him what I am experiencing. After speaking with Dr. Snyder, he tells me to come right to his office. Jack drives me there. I tell Dr. Snyder I am feeling sweaty and nauseous and have a pounding headache. He immediately orders a lithium level. I go to the lab to have the blood test. Dr. Snyder orders it stat.

He says to go home and stay there and that he will call me as soon as he has the results of the lithium level, which will be around 6 p.m. Jack and I wait together for the call. Dr. Snyder calls at 5:30 p.m. and says my lithium level is above the high normal and that I need to pack a bag and meet him at the hospital. That is the psychiatric hospital. That is the only type of hospital he has privileges at. Oh no, not this again! I hope this isn't a recipe to lose Jack.

Dr. Snyder explains on the phone, which by the way is unusual. Usually he doesn't explain anything, he just barks orders. He says that my level is too high to not to be under observation; that observation is the safest thing for me now. So there I go back in the psychiatric hospital. My mother seems ok with all this, not surprising.

Jack knows about my past and he is aware of the toxicity and hospitalizations. But he has not been through any of it with me. That is the hard part. I can't have any visitors while under observation, except my immediate family. That doesn't do me much good. Jack is 5' 10" and has the handsomest, square jaw I'd seen on anyone, just like Tom Selleck. I worry; I hope he can handle all this.

My mother visits me. It always feels like she thinks she has to, not that she really wants to. My father is always at work and so are my brothers. I remain in the hospital for over a week, with them poking me every day for additional lithium levels, until Dr. Snyder sees that my levels are normal.

I am still too young to understand the ramifications of both the lithium toxicities. I know that the second one seems less severe. As far as the symptoms, the second time around I do not have those mind-altering hallucinations. I am thankful for that.

*

The day I get home, Jack comes to visit me. He brings flowers and is very happy to see me. We embrace, and I am the one who is so happy. He is there for me. He is not walking away from our relationship, not yet at least. His mother and father cannot have been happy about my hospitalization. They know it is a psychiatric hospital. They really do not accept me as a permanent fixture in Jack's life yet.

It did convince me of one thing. Jack really does have a backbone. He is making his own decisions about our relationship and loves me and isn't going to walk away. Even during a challenging time.

The next time I am at Jack's house for dinner, it is the first time I see his parents since arriving home from the psych ward. They don't act differently towards me, not at all. It seems odd, until I realize that they are probably in denial about my health, the same way my parents are.

*

Jack and I go away every month for one weekend, always within driving distance of our homes. His mother hates this and encourages us to marry already. On the other hand, my mother whispers to me before I leave the house, "Do you have your birth control pills?"

We often double date with John and his new girlfriend Sheryl. She is very sure of herself, and that intimidates me. She knows exactly what she wants and goes after it. We go to Canada on the train with them. Jack and John think it is a good idea to bring a fifth of vodka with us. One of them makes the mistake of taking it out of the bag to show us what brand it is. The conductor sees the bottle and takes it away from us and that is the end of that.

About a year after my most recent hospital stay, Jack proposes to me—and I accept.

21

Jack has family in Florida. We visit them a couple of times. One time we fly to Orlando to go to Disney World and then drive to see his relatives. It is Jack's mother's sister who lives there. She has three grown daughters, and they all have children as well.

Jack's oldest cousin, Jim, has three children, all younger than Jack. Jack appeals to Jim for a job. Jack has a degree in accounting and is about to sit for his CPA exam. Jim is a shrewd businessman and sees how eager Jack is to get a job and get out from under the thumb of his parents. And why not leave the Midwest winters behind for Florida?!

After we return home, Jim calls Jack and offers him a job at the racetrack where he owns concessions stands. Jack jumps at the offer. They speak at great length about the job description and when he has to be there, in Florida. All we need to do is move the wedding date up. Originally we plan on a late spring date; we now change it to January. Right smack dab in the middle of a Midwestern winter.

My mother is not too happy about any of this for many reasons. First, me moving to Florida is out of her realm of thinking. Actually, moving anywhere out of the Midwest is not in her realm of thinking. When Jack and I break the news to my parents, it is as if someone has just been in a tragic accident or worse. Florida is a three-hour plane ride from the Midwest.

For many nights, more than I can count, my mother goes to bed crying. Not only do I have the nerve to move up my wedding, I am leaving her; she will lose control over me. As usual, it is all about her.

My mother shares with me that she saw my grandmother at the assisted living that day. My mother told my grandmother that Jack accepted a job offer and we are moving up the wedding and going to live in Florida after we marry, and how miserable she is about it.

My grandmother tells her to stop and realize that she will be able to call me or mail me cards or letters. Along with Jack and I visiting them in the Midwest and my dad and her visiting us in Florida. "After all," she says, "when I left home in Europe, I never had that option or benefit, Sally. You need to think about that." It is a profound moment for both of them.

My mother backs down somewhat, meaning she isn't crying every night anymore. But as time goes on and I move to Florida, every time we visit one another, a lot of drama does ensue. If Jack and I fly in from Florida to the Midwest for a visit, and when my parents drop us back at the airport, my mother starts crying in the car. It is contagious; I start crying and both of us are a mess.

It bothers me and makes me uncomfortable hearing her cry and whine about me moving on, but somewhere, down deep, I know this is going to be one of the best things that happens to me. Getting out of the clutches of my mother's hold, the constant smothering and intrusive questioning. I am 21 and more than ready to fly away.

22

I am busy attending to all the details that require one's attention when having a wedding. I am going to have seven bridesmaids— my three sisters-in-law, Jack's two sisters-in-law and my two best friends, Lynn and Chris.

We are at a bridal shop and all hell breaks loose. My sisters-in-law Lois and Jean want nothing to do with my wedding. They are taking my Maid of Honor, Lynn, aside and trying to convince her to change my mind on the choice of bridesmaid dresses.

Lois is married to my oldest brother Lee. Jean is married to my middle brother Miles. Lois and Jean really don't like each other. But ganging up and making my life miserable is a favorite pastime of theirs. They were in the same high school class and in rival cliques.

Lynn is trying on bridesmaid gowns at the bridal shop for my wedding. Lois and Jean, my warring sisters-in-law, corner Lynn with several selections of their own for her to try on, and then try to convince me to pick one of the ones that they like best. That isn't happening anytime soon. I go with my original choice, which is a dark purple long gown. The dress is a classic style and will be great as a cocktail dress, once cut shorter.

Lois and Jean have other ideas. They have no trouble letting me know that they hate the dress, period. They will suffer through and wear it at my wedding to Jack. They tell me that the morning after my wedding the dress is going into a box for Goodwill. That is fine with me.

My wedding gown has a sweetheart neckline. It is light ivory. It has tiny buttons up the back that start at my waistline. The train is quite long. They have to give Lynn specific instructions of how to attach the train to my gown after the ceremony.

Lynn has a bridal shower for me at her parents' home. It is on a Sunday afternoon. There are about two dozen people there. Lynn invites my closest friends, along with my mother, future mother-in-law, two future sisters-in-law and my three sisters-in-law.

A luncheon is first. There is spinach, tomato quiche, egg soufflé, a large tossed salad and a fruit platter. Everything is homemade by Lynn's mom. She is an excellent cook and a gracious host. Strawberry shortcake is for dessert with tea and coffee.

The gifts consist of an assortment of personal items that a new bride will love. A teddy or two, satin nightgowns, a peignoir set from my mother (she takes me shopping to be sure it is the exact one I want). That is nice of her. It is white satin with white lace, very sheer and beautiful.

Lynn and my friends Mary and Chris give me a jewelry box with five drawers, and the top of the box opens to find slots for rings and small treasures. I also receive several different kinds of bubble bath, moisturizer and perfumes. Channel N° 5 is my favorite, and I receive that as well.

Jack and I register at the local department store. The popular colors are burgundy, gray and mauve. We register for sheets and towels in these colors, along with the other essential items: dishes, glassware, flatware, pots and pans and small appliances.

We also pick out our china pattern. It comes from England; I want something with classic lines that is simple but elegant. The pattern has a solid gold rim around the edge of the plates. Along with an inner gold ring, the china consists of a small floral pattern in dark royal blue, with touches of burgundy, and then has a gold lattice over the design, so beautiful and just right.

My in-laws want to buy us our china for our shower gift. They have some connections in Ontario, Canada. They place an order for a dozen seven-piece place settings. It is customary to receive five-piece place settings. Jack's parents want me to have the extra two pieces, the soup and dessert dishes that will be nice for entertaining.

There is one catch. His parents want to pay for half of the china. And ask me to pay for the other half. After thinking it over I agree since they are getting a 50% discount as well. Jack and I and his folks drive though the Windsor tunnel to Canada a few months later, when the china arrives from England.

Lois, Jean and Bonnie, my three sisters-in-law, also have a bridal shower for me. I am happy they are all getting along right now. It is at a restaurant near home, the Melting Pot, a fondue restaurant that is delicious. There are over sixty people there, all of our relatives, friends of mine, friends of my mother's and future mother-in-law, along with my grandmother. She is the only grandparent left on either side of our families.

Jack and I receive almost everything we registered for. Lynn makes me the traditional bow bouquet to use at our wedding rehearsal. A bow bouquet is when you take a paper plate and cut a hole in the center of it and slip the ribbons from the gifts though the hole. The result is all the beautiful bows from our gifts bulging out of the plate.

After the gifts are open, Jack, my dad and future father-in-law show up to share in the pleasure of the day. It is wonderful having so many people that love us in one room. At the end of the shower the men help pack everything up and take it to my house to repack to ship to Florida.

23

The snow is coming down slowly, white flakes covering all the trees, a beautiful winter day for a wedding. It is a lovely ceremony and there are over two hundred people there. The reception room is stunning, with purple and white flowers as centerpieces and white tablecloths with purple napkins. The room is glowing with candlelight.

Jack and I are having a wonderful time. We have just cut the wedding cake and feed each other a piece, you know, in the messy way, shoving it into each other's mouths. We can't eat much more than the cake, we are so excited about our future. We make sure to take the opportunity to thank all our guests for making it such a special day. Then we dance the night away.

We go to San Juan, Puerto Rico, for our honeymoon. We stay at a high-rise hotel on the beach. The weather is perfect, eighty degrees every day and sunny. We drink Pina Coladas while spending lazy days on chaises at the beach.

A week later, we fly home. We ship our shower and wedding gifts to Florida. We had flown down in July of 1979, to find an apartment prior to the wedding. Hurricanes are a concern of ours. Hurricane David hit South Florida early in September 1979. Jack and I are safe and sound in the Midwest and are glad to be moving to Florida after hurricane season.

It seems like a great idea, so there you have it, in mid-January 1980, Jack and I move into our first home together. The condo is on the second floor of a four-story building. There is an elevator. We seldom use that, and instead, we take the stairs to the catwalk which leads to our front door.

After living there a few days we meet some of our neighbors, stopping the elevator for a few moments to put all their groceries, packages, etc. on the elevator and then start it back up to their appropriate floor. We continue to take the steps, packages or not. It is great exercise.

After unpacking and organizing our things in our new home, it is time for me to find a job. My last position in the Midwest was as an office manager for two internists who shared space with three other doctors. It was a fast-paced practice and I enjoyed the work. What made it even more interesting was sharing the space with three other doctors and their staff. It still was sometimes hard for me to get respect since I was only 22, and had a great deal of responsibility. My job included training staff to do clerical work, along with how to file insurance claims, and work with the doctors and help with the patients. I was sad to leave this thriving practice when Jack and I married and moved to Florida. The doctors gave me a glowing reference, which assisted me in finding a new position in Florida.

The first two interviews are for small practices. That isn't appealing to me. I keep looking. I come across an ad for three young internists that are opening a new practice. They are looking for an office manager. I apply for the job and get it.

24

As a result of the three young internists just starting out, they are not looking for full-time staff. I work there about thirty to thirty-five hours a week. This leaves me plenty of time to do laundry, keep our condo clean, and have dinner ready for Jack when he gets home.

I really am not very good at heavy cleaning, washing floors, bathrooms, vacuuming, etc. Actually, I don't have a clue, because my mother did not teach me. She let Susan do the cleaning and always told me not to bother because I didn't do a good job. I just turn 23, am a newlywed in a new city with plenty of my new husband's family nearby, but none of my own. It is embarrassing having to ask them any kind of domestic questions.

One day, I fill a new bucket with a gallon of water and a half cup each of bleach and ammonia. Then put my new sponge mop in the bucket and squeeze out the excess liquid. Using lots of pressure, I push the mop down on the floor and scrub. I can see the difference almost immediately. The floor looks lighter in color, cleaner, fresher and the vinyl flooring shines.

It is strange; I really am not exerting that much effort or energy to wash the floor, but I start coughing, feel dizzy and find it a little difficult to breathe. It is a warm day and the air conditioning is on. Opening the window in the kitchen seems to be the best idea at the moment. Standing by the window I try to take long deep breaths until my lungs begin to clear and I stop coughing.

The adventure of cleaning my kitchen floor that day comes to an end. I think it is best to get out of the kitchen and lie down on the couch in the living room for a while. Soon after, Jack gets home. It isn't normal seeing me lying on the couch that time of day and he wonders what is wrong.

I tell him that I was cleaning the kitchen floor; and that I mixed the ammonia and bleach with the water. Jack is immediately upset. It appears he knows more about cleaning products than I do, and tells me that mixing bleach and ammonia makes chlorine gas, which is highly dangerous. It was used as a chemical weapon during WW I and WW II, quite a learning experience.

It seems to me that I am better off working out of the home environment. and am glad to return to the office and take my role on as office manager there. Parts of my responsibilities are to help the group advertise and build their practice. That takes time and patience. And the doctors introduce themselves to other doctors in the building and the hospitals they have an affiliation with.

Things go smoothly. and over time that is just what happens for the doctors. They become busier week by week. My three bosses suggest that I call them by their first names, providing there are not any patients in the office. This is new to me and I did not feel totally comfortable with the idea, but soon it becomes natural.

*

One day at work I notice that I am having trouble urinating and that my stomach is very swollen. Someone might have mistaken me for being pregnant, and that's how bad it is. At 5 p.m., I feel I have no choice but to ask Michael, one of the doctors I am working for, for help. I explain how I am feeling and at that point can no longer bear the pain in my abdomen.

It isn't pleasant and I find it embarrassing, but there is no other choice, since it is now close to eight hours since I was able to urinate. It is necessary, and my embarrassment soon passes, because the reality is that someone has to help stop the pain. I trust Michael; it is a good choice under the circumstances.

He instructs me to go right into exam room five and wait for him. While he gathers a catheter and other sterile equipment, I am lying down on the examination table with my knees bent and my feet at the very edge of the table. He is going to catheterize me. My boss gently inserts the plastic tube, known as the urinary catheter, into my bladder via my urethra. This allows my urine to drain freely into a container allowing my bladder to empty. I immediately have some relief.

After the catheterization process, my boss calls the urologist on the third floor of our medical building. His name is Karl Smyth, MD. Fortunately for me, Dr. Smyth is still in his office and he tells Michael to bring me upstairs to his office immediately. Dr. Smyth stands well over six feet and resembles Mr. Clean, with a bald shiny head and a smile that melts your heart.

He asks to examine me. Dr. Smyth is a gentle soul and very kind to me. He tells me he has to admit me to the hospital for extensive testing to find out why I cannot urinate. At this point I call Jack at work. This happens so suddenly, it is frightening. Especially, the why part; why is this happening and how long is it going to last?

The hospital is next to the medical building. Dr. Smyth walks me over to the hospital, and personally escorts me to admitting. Walking into the admitting office with this well-known urologist is a stroke of luck for me. The paperwork, etc. is done in less than ten minutes and they whisk me off to a hospital room.

Jack leaves work after I contact him and stops at our condo to pack a small bag of toiletries, a nightgown and a robe. He arrives at the hospital around 8 p.m. and stays with me until the nurses kick him out at 11 p.m. He has not been able to meet Dr. Smyth yet. Jack plans on coming back to the hospital early in the morning, prior to any of the tests I am going to have, so he can meet the doctor.

Dr. Smyth orders a cystoscopy for the next morning. It is a procedure to see inside the bladder and the urethra. It is not a pleasant test. A cystoscope is a special tube with a small camera on the end of it. I have to lie flat on my back on a hard, rigid table, with my knees up and apart. The procedure takes about fifteen minutes, which feels more like two hours.

Dr. Smyth explains everything about the procedure as he is doing it. I find this to be a great comfort. My experience is that most doctors do not do this. Dr. Smyth understands that talking the patient through the procedure helps keep the anxiety and stress level down.

First. they cleanse the urethra. The water is very cold. Next, is applying local anesthetic to the area, then the insertion of the scope through the urethra into the bladder. then the insertion of water or saline through the cystoscope to fill the bladder. As Dr. Smyth is doing this, he asks me to describe the feeling. He explains my answers will help reveal information about my condition, so that he can make a diagnosis and treatment plan. As he injects the fluid, it stretches my bladder walls, letting him see the entire bladder. This is the hardest and most uncomfortable part.

Once Dr. Smyth says the procedure is over, he drains my bladder and removes the tube. This part isn't painful at all, since I am still numb from the local anesthetic. The nurse helps me off the exam table and takes me back to my room on a stretcher. I rest in my hospital room for the remainder of the day. Dr. Smyth tells me that he will see me the next morning with the test results.

Jack visits that evening. He stops by Subway and picks me up a meatball sub. It is delicious; everyone knows that hospital food isn't very appealing, let alone appetizing. He shares the events of his day with me. We are both anxious to find out what the results of the cystoscopy are.

Bright and early at 7:30 a.m., Dr. Smyth comes into my room—along with his wonderful personality. You know he cares about you as a person, not just another patient. He tells me he has good news and bad news; I choose to hear the good news first.

Dr. Smyth feels that my diagnosis is the good news, always a positive guy. He says I have a neurogenic bladder. A neurogenic bladder is when the bladder does not empty properly due to a neurological condition. Dr. Smyth knows my medical history; he had asked about it the day Michael took me to his office. He is well aware of the lithium toxicities, and believes that the second toxicity is the cause of the neurogenic bladder. I have my parents to thank, blame, for this. Why did they allow me to have another toxicity? Why were they not paying attention? And what was Dr. Snyder thinking?

Dr. Smyth prescribes a medication, Urecholine. He says I need to take it for a year, and that I will be able to reverse most of the damage that the toxicity left me with. The medication helps me to urinate and empty my bladder. He explains that the toxicity causes the muscle in the bladder to not allow it to empty completely. Therefore, the residual urine stays in the bladder and causes infections, and in my case total bladder failure.

I will also need to be on Macrodatin, which is an antibiotic to help ward off any future urinary tract infections, while the Urecholine will help the bladder muscles recover, so that I can be emptying my bladder completely. I am not happy about having to be on an antibiotic for a long period of time, but I understand why.

The bad news, Dr. Smyth says, is that I cannot get pregnant at this time, as my bladder will not be able to support a baby during pregnancy. He thinks I will have to wait two years.

I am 23 with total bladder failure, a newlywed living in a new and strange city. Some common causes of a neurogenic bladder are stroke, spinal cord injury, multiple sclerosis, and in patients with diabetic neuropathy to name a few, but mine was "only" due to the lithium toxicity—and my parents' inattention to what was happening to me when I was younger. Dr. Smyth has such a charismatic, down-to-earth and caring way that I feel so fortunate to find a doctor who will help me with my recovery and rebuilding and reclaiming my body.

Jack is unable to be at the hospital that morning. He has pressing business to attend to at work. Somehow that does not sit well with me, considering how serious of a medical problem I am facing. I feel alone at a time when I should not.

Strange how things happen. Even though Jack and I are newlyweds and he is ready for children, I do not think I am. We are both going through many life changes. Being newlyweds is certainly one, moving to a new city and becoming familiar with it is hard enough. Thinking about having a baby right away seems like a bad idea. We are young and have our whole lives ahead of us. I know I can overcome this situation and do want children. But will my marriage survive until my bladder recovers?

I am able to leave the hospital late that afternoon. Jack picks me up to take me home. When he arrives at the hospital he seems cheerful and happy that I am going home. I ask him to sit down and I explain everything. I can see he is physically and emotionally shaken. It is a real blow to him having to wait to start a family. It seems to me that his mother is pushing him, for us to get pregnant right away and start a large family that she wants us to have.

25

I take a leave of absence from my job. I need to recover and get familiar with the medication schedule. Dr. Smyth sees me every week for the first couple of months, and then once a month thereafter for the entire year. I know the drill after only a couple of visits.

First Dr. Smyth calls me into his office. I feel safe in his office. He has four children, and they are all beautiful, two boys and two girls, two in middle school and two in high school. He has pictures of them all over his office, along with pictures of his lovely wife, and of course his many diplomas.

Dr. Smyth always makes me feel like he has all the time in the world to talk to me. He starts by asking how I am feeling, if I am in any pain or if I have pain while urinating. For the most part my answers are no pain and feeling better every day. Next, Dr. Smyth asks me to stop in the restroom and empty my bladder and then go to the exam room. He instructs me to push gently on my bladder to help it empty completely. Pressing lightly on my bladder and being patient will ensure it is empty.

After that, I go into the examination room and undress from the waist down. I put on a paper gown and have a sheet to cover myself as well. Dr. Smyth knocks on the door and comes into the room with his nurse Nancy. He asks me to lie down on the table and bend my knees, so that he can catheterize me, by sticking a needle into my bladder through my urethra.

Dr. Smyth is very gentle. Again, he always lets me know what he is doing as he is doing it. This remains a great comfort. He then immediately reports how much urine he collects. Sometimes it is 8cc's, sometimes 10cc's, and as my bladder muscle heals it goes down to 4cc's or less.

The reason Dr. Smyth has to catheterize me every time I have an office visit with him is to determine how quickly and how well I am recovering. He needs to know how much residual urine I am holding in my bladder. That also explains why he wants me to empty my bladder as much as possible on my own, prior to him catheterizing me.

Dr. Smyth is always encouraging and hopeful about my recovery. He says I need to have an overabundance of patience during this time. The fact that I am so young when I have total bladder failure is rare, yet is clearly because of the lithium toxicity. He has faith in me that I will continue to improve and be able to have a baby in the future.

Jack is not as positive. He really wants me to be pregnant now. That is not how the cards are playing out. He will need to be patient and supportive during my recovery; I know it is hard for him.

*

I had not had much experience with sex prior to dating Jack. Our sex life seems normal the four years we date. There is plenty of time to be alone and intimate. We are very much in love and our priority is pleasing each other.

After our honeymoon and settling into our new life, making love seems to have fallen by the wayside; at times it feels like Jack is more of a brother than a husband. He likes to smoke pot and has been smoking it for years with his brother Mark and friends. Jack asks me to try smoking pot with him and I did try it a couple of times, but really hate smoke.

Jack comes home from the office and the first thing he does after changing out of his work clothes is to smoke a joint. Keep in mind we did not live together prior to marriage. What a mistake. If we had, things may have been different.

I make dinner, and he always has a great appetite, which is no surprise after getting high. We have a pleasant enough dinner and then he zones out in front of the TV. I clean the dishes and join him for a while. TV really does not interest me very much, so I get a book and join Jack on the couch and usually fall asleep there.

Upon waking, I am alone. Jack does not wake me before he goes to bed. There is a real disconnect here. This goes on night after night during the week, never going to bed together. The real lack of intimacy grows. I approach Jack about this, and it does not seem to bother him too much. We make love on the weekends, which he says is enough for him. I think this odd for a couple in their early twenties. Again, I have nothing to compare this to and no one in my circle of friends really to talk to about this kind of intimacy.

I guess that the main reason this is going on, or going wrong, depending how you look at it, is because his parents were all over about us about going away for weekends together. They did not approve of this prior to our marriage. So now that we are married, it is no longer something rebellious. In other words, now that it is "legal," it isn't as much of an interest to Jack.

Then things get a bit uglier. About two weeks after I return to our new home after getting out of the hospital, Jack receives a call from his parents. We know that his parents always plan to retire to Florida at some point, so my mother-in-law can be close to her sister and nieces and great nieces and nephews.

Both his mother and father make a promise that they will wait at least a full year, giving us time to be alone that first year of our marriage. My mother-in-law tells Jack that they have just sold their house. They have hired a moving van and it is coming the next day to bring all their furniture and other belongings to Florida. No, they don't have a house yet, but they plan on staying with his mom's sister Frances in her three-bedroom condo until they find a house.

They will put all their things in storage. My in-laws are leaving in two days, and driving straight through to Florida, each driving their own car, following each other on the highway.

My mother-in-law is the youngest of five children. She is not demonstrative in any way. As a matter of fact, when we greet each other, she prefers to just say "hi" across the room. I will give her a hug anyway, but she never returns it.

I do not have experience with anyone like her. Cold and calculating, she certainly doesn't want to share her son with me or anyone. Jack is a mama's boy. It is unfortunate that I did not figure this out sooner.

Once they settle in Florida; that is settle in at Ellen's sister's home, we go to dinner there every Friday night. It is mandatory. Dinner at Jack's aunt's apartment is fine. She is a pleasant person, nothing like her younger sister. It seems impossible to have two siblings be so very different.

Aunt Frances has three daughters and Ellen has three sons. Possibly this is the difference. I'm not sure. Aunt Frances is a good cook and I enjoy being with all the cousins.

Jack and I love following the TV show *Dallas*. It is one of the few TV shows I watch with him. If we don't go home by nine o'clock we miss it. And it isn't an option to watch it at Jack's aunt's house. My father-in-law, Wally, always has a problem with this. He gives us a glaring look as we bid our good-byes to everyone. He often takes Jack aside to scold him about us being the first to leave. We have been there for almost three hours and dinner and dessert have been done for more than an hour now. We decide to leave anyway. Since this doesn't please my father-in-law, we are in the doghouse with him, too.

26

Interestingly enough, my parents and my in-laws are looking for a home at the same time. It has always been a dream of my father's to move to Florida when he retires, and my parents want to purchase a home in advance. So off they all go to find a home.

In the early 1980s, communities are going up all over Florida. One of the communities is being built near Jack and me. This is a boom time for real estate. One literally has to stand in line for hours to get their name on a list because only a certain number of homes are available in each phase of building. Once the buyer meets the financial requirements, they get an approval call and letter. Then you pick from a plan which lot you want and which elevation you like. *Elevation* meaning what the front of your new home will look like. The floor plan might be the same for three different elevations.

While visiting us, my parents look at many communities and are sold on one. Being a community there are lots of attractive amenities, such as a pool, clubhouse, tennis courts, walking trails and maintenance. There is a monthly association fee, which allows you to use the amenities, and not worry about the maintenance of the property.

My parents and Jack's parents each pick out a lot in the same community, understanding that there are only a hundred homes built in each phase. The type of home that both our parents are trying to buy is a village home. And of the hundred homes built, there are two-bedroom and three-bedroom models. It is first-come, first served. You have two or three lots to choose from. That is it.

As it turns out, my parents and in-laws are going to live four doors away from each other on the same block. My parents do not have much in common with Jack's. And especially after the stories I share with them about how cold Jack's mom is, they do not have much interest in being neighbors.

My parents fly back to the Midwest and I have power of attorney for them. When the final papers are ready for their new home, I will be signing all the papers.

I am at work and get a phone call from the developer. They tell me that a lot has become available on a cul-de-sac, two blocks away from the original lot they now have near my in-laws. The cul-de-sac is being built next to a man-made lake; the backyard will be facing the lake. The lot costs $1000 more, and they have forty-eight hours to decide if they want it. My parents are higher on the list than my in-laws; therefore, getting first choice. I call them immediately and my mom discusses it with my dad and calls me back. It is a big yes! They are so happy about it.

27

Soon after my parents and in-laws close on their properties, I find a lump in my right breast. It feels a bit larger than a green pea, and it is hard.

When I was 16 my mother was hospitalized for a biopsy on one of her breasts. This was another incident where I was kept in the dark, at least semi-dark. My whole family, my father and three brothers and I, were gathered around my mother's hospital bed. It was almost as if we were just waiting for the clergy to read my mother the last rites. Instead, the surgeon came into the room with papers on a clipboard for my mother to sign.

At this point, my brothers ushered me out the door, as the doctor was going to explain what the papers said. According to my family and the way they overprotected me, it was time for me to leave and not hear what the doctor had to say about the documents that my mother had to sign before her surgery.

It turns out the papers stated that if during surgery, a tumor or cancer was found, my mother was giving the surgeon permission to remove her breast if necessary. I was more than old enough to understand what was going on. And it was overkill to remove me from the room. It only made me think of worse things, like the surgeon already knew he had to do more extensive surgery or that she didn't have long to live.

They had to intubate my mother and put her under anesthesia. To intubate means placing a tube into an internal orifice (your throat) to allow the body to continue breathing. Being put under is always a frightening thing to me. What if you don't wake up, or wake up and you are different for the rest of your life?

That wasn't the case for my mother. She woke up and she was the same old person except that she had anxiety waiting for the result of the biopsy. I could understand that. Fortunately, the biopsy came back showing no cancer. It did show that she had fibrocystic disease, lumpiness and usually discomfort in one or both breasts. The condition is very common and usually benign, meaning that fibrocystic breasts are not malignant; in other words, the condition is not cancerous.

I became familiar with this whole process. This was not the only time that my mother would go through this. She had several other surgeries along with mammograms every year. There was no cancer found. But lots of anxiety until each and every test result was received.

My sister-in-law Jean, my brother Miles' wife, had a staph infection in one of her breasts a couple months prior to me finding the lump in mine. A staph infection of the breast is caused by bacteria that enter the breast through a break in the skin or the nipple. This often happens during breastfeeding. Jean was hospitalized for this infection and treated with antibiotics.

After a week of the treatment, the doctors said that the infection was not completely cured, and they opted for surgery. So Jean had to have a portion of her breast tissue removed from one breast in order to remove the infected area. A few days later she was discharged from the hospital and had a complete recovery at home.

Freaking out, I want this lump gone before it gets any larger, and sure want to know that it isn't cancer. I call my internist who refers me to a surgeon, Dr. Neil Kennedy. I call for a consultation.

When I arrive at the office, I fill out the new-patient information form and then wait and wait and wait. Unfortunately, surgeons can often be late for their office patients, because they are late finishing surgeries they perform in the mornings. This is something you just need to understand in advance and have a lot of patience waiting your turn. I do have a book with me, but find it hard to concentrate.

Finally, after over ninety minutes—and yes the office staff does communicate to the patients waiting to be seen that the doctor is running late— finally they take me into the exam room. The nurse asks me to remove my shirt and bra and put the shapeless gown on with the opening in the front.

Dr. Kennedy is a warm, down-to-earth man. He isn't very tall, has brown eyes and gray hair and wears glasses. He examines my breasts and asks me if I have ever had a mammogram. My answer is no, I am only 24 years old. He orders a mammogram and tells me he isn't sure that it will be helpful in diagnosing what the lump is, but it will be the first step.

Since I never have had a mammogram before, I am apprehensive. The appointment is later this week, only two days after my visit with the surgeon. Women tell me that mammograms hurt, especially if you have small breasts. Because the machine pinches your breast tissue together to take the x-rays, the technician actually has you stand very tall in front of the machine, and uses her hand to push your breast into the shelf-like metal area. She tells me to hold my breath and that the pinching does not last too long. The tech moves away from the machine to an area of the room that has the controls that she needs to operate it and to take a picture, which comes out on x-ray film.

Next thing I know, I feel like my eyes are going to pop out of my head. It seems like minutes not seconds until she comes back over to the mammogram machine where I am standing to release my breast from the grip of the machine. What a relief, until I realize that she is only half done with the test; now the process will start all over again for the other breast.

I see Dr. Kennedy for an office visit the next day in order to get the results of the mammogram. The nurse takes me into Dr. Kennedy's private office. He says that the mammogram is not conclusive, and he recommends removing the lump, a lumpectomy to be exact. It is an outpatient procedure, a day surgery. After the surgery, I will go home from the hospital with pain medication, and see him for a postoperative office visit to get the results of the biopsy.

Jack is supportive. He says he understands how frightening it must be for a woman to have this kind of surgery. I am trying to look at it from a positive point of view; at least I found the lump when it is small, and I am in the hands of an excellent surgeon, who also has a kind and gentle bedside manner. This is not always the case. What I learned early on working in the medical field is that you pick a surgeon because he/she has a great track record. Good bedside manner is a bonus, not a requirement.

My parents are still living in the Midwest at the time and Jack has to go to work that day, for a special meeting. He arranges a ride to the hospital for me with one of his cousins. That is a bit uncomfortable for me. I ask Jack if he can possibly miss the meeting. He says that is impossible. Considering he works for his cousin-in-law, I have a hard time understanding this.

Early in the morning the day of the surgery, Jack's cousin, his boss' wife Molly, picks me up at the condo and drives me to the hospital. She lets me off at the door that says "Admissions and Day Surgery." I feel deserted, alone and scared.

The nurse asks me to change into a surgical gown and robe, removing all my clothes and placing them into a locker, along with my purse and shoes. They also supply me with those sock type of booties with the nonskid bottoms. The nurse starts an IV in my left arm. At least she tries, and on the second attempt finds a vein. This is very painful. She isn't able to start it from the inside of my elbow, and on the second and successful attempt, she uses the top of my hand, where the skin is very thin. Ouch!

The anesthesiologist comes by to say hello and tells me that he is going to put medication into the IV line to help me relax, and will be moving me into the operating room in the next fifteen minutes. It is 7:30 a.m., and the doctor is true to his word and at 7:45 a.m. they wheel my gurney out of the preoperative area into the operating room. I do not remember anything after that.

I wake up in the recovery area and the nurse that is attending to me, asks me how I am feeling and if I want something to drink. I have some apple juice and graham crackers while sitting up on the gurney. The recovery nurse tells me that I will need to stay there for at least thirty more minutes. She asks me if I have anyone waiting for me in the surgical waiting room. I say no, and ask her if she can call my cousin who is going to pick me up.

Jack's cousin Molly arrives to take me back to her house about an hour later. None of us feel comfortable with the idea of me being alone at the condo. I am grateful for that. I spend the rest of the day lounging with Molly.

Being proactive, I have the prescription for pain medication with me. I take one pill when we arrive at Molly's house. Three hours later; it is late afternoon, and I am not feeling very well. The pain isn't the problem, it is nausea. And then comes the vomiting. It is time to call the surgeon. I am not able to keep any food or liquids down. He suspects that the pain medication is causing the problem, and he instructs me to come right to the emergency room and will need to stay in the hospital for observation overnight. I am not too happy about this and neither is Molly, as Jack is coming to pick me up in a couple of hours and take me home.

Molly calls her sister Eileen and asks her to drive me to the ER, since Molly isn't able to. I'll never forget this car ride. Eileen has a Cadillac convertible. It is pale yellow with a black top and lots of extras. She lives only two blocks away from her sister. She pulls up to Molly's house and honks the horn. I go out to her car and she speeds to the hospital. I feel like a ragdoll being thrown around. It isn't as if I am dying or anything; she just doesn't want me throwing up in her car. She hands me a bag to use if I have to throw up. Who can blame her?

The emergency room doctor is aware that I am coming in. They take me to a hospital room for the night. They have to start another IV, and I am so out of it, I do not notice the pain. The nurse hangs a bag from my IV pole that looks like water. She tells me that the doctor says I need hydration, and they are forcing liquids through my IV, which will make me feel better.

They take me on a gurney and two of the orderlies lift me with the sheets by my head and feet and gently put me on to the hospital bed. They only have private rooms at this hospital. The rooms are in a pie shape slice, with the head of the bed being at the widest part of the pie and your feet pointing to the window. It is actually quite pleasant looking out the window at the beautiful greenery, instead of looking at the hospital corridor.

Jack arrives sometime in the evening; I lose track of time. He tells me he feels awful that I got sick at his cousin's house. He has a meatball sub for me, my favorite at the time. The problem is I am not holding down food very well. I encourage him to eat it.

Jack stays for a while and then goes home to go to sleep. He wants to stay and sleep on the lounge chair that is in the hospital room. I insist he needs a good night's sleep at home so he will be fresh in the morning for work. However, I do remind him that there is a strong possibility that I will be able to come home in the morning. He suggests that I call one of his cousins to pick me up.

Once, again, it is disappointing, Jack's lack of devotion. After all, we are partners, taking this journey through life together for better or worse. I am beginning to realize that finding a lump in my breast is a real inconvenience for Jack, a thorn in his side.

Six days later, I drive by myself to Dr. Kennedy's office for the results of the biopsy from my lumpectomy. The lump is benign, thankfully no cancer. It is fibrocystic disease. The same thing my mother has. Dr. Kennedy apologizes for putting me through the surgery, but that is the only way to find out what the lump is, fortunately with such a good outcome.

28

Life moves along for Jack and me. It seems like I already have two strikes against me since we moved to Florida. First, total bladder failure, then having to go through the lumpectomy. And there is more to come.

One of the doctors who I am working for is adamant about getting to the bottom of why I have total bladder failure at the age of 23. He shows genuine concern and takes the view that not all doctors stick together. And he wants all the details that lead up to the bladder failure.

I share the whole story with him, explaining the details of the lithium toxicity and all the problems that followed and that my parents never discuss consequences of their choices. Michael asks me how long it has been since the last time I have seen Dr. Snyder. He wants to be sure it is less than six years ago, because of the statute of limitations. The law requires that a medical malpractice lawsuit be filed within two years of the injury, or within six months of discovery to a maximum of six years following the date of the injury. In my case of permanent organ damage, it has been just a month since I have total bladder failure, and less than six years since I last saw the doctor. Michael tells me I have to be quick about filing the lawsuit prior to the six years, and to get in touch with an attorney as soon as possible.

That night after work, I go home and make calls to my brothers. I am thinking that they will help me. I call Lee first. He tells me that he has a family friend that is an attorney, who can help find a malpractice attorney for me. That is a successful call. I then place a call to Miles asking him if he can rent a car for me. He says he is busy with dinner and can't help me. No surprise there. Warren and Bonnie are living far from home, so I don't call them.

Jack arrives home soon after I make the calls. I explain to him what Michael told me about suing Dr. Snyder, and the statute of limitations in regards to the lawsuit. I tell him I want to fly home next week. He says he doesn't want me to go alone and wants to go with me. I am happy to hear this. We can't stay at my parents' house, because when I call them and tell them what is happening my mother tells me that I shouldn't take on this type of challenge, that I am not strong enough to handle it. And I will not be able to stay at their house. This does not surprise me; actually, she is the one who can't handle it. She has her head in the sand, denial as usual.

Jack contacts his parents who are home getting the house ready to sell, and they are glad to have us stay with them. My in-laws are surprisingly supportive and don't ask too many questions. They said they are sorry to hear that I have to go through so much, and understand why I am taking this upon myself to accomplish. That is a relief.

We fly home on the Monday of Memorial Day week. My appointment with the attorney is on Tuesday morning at 8:30. Jack's parents pick us up at the airport. We sleep in Jack's old room. It is kind of strange and comforting at the same time.

The next morning, we leave at 8 a.m. sharp to meet the attorney. Jack uses his father's car. My brother Lee is meeting us there as well. Lee is the only one from my family who is supporting me.

The attorney's name is Joe Goodwin. I had sent Mr. Goodwin my medical records, prior to meeting with him, along with the "brown envelope."

Before moving to Florida my best friend Lynn and I went to Dr. Snyder's office together. Lynn was there for support; she always was. Her compassion, understanding, anger on my behalf and devotion to our friendship were never-ending. We walked in shoulder to shoulder and approached the front desk.

On more occasions than I can remember, I asked Dr. Snyder what was in the brown envelope. It was a large envelope, 8½ by 10½ and clasped in my chart with my other records and test results. I knew this was odd that he had not removed the papers from the envelope and inserted them into the chart like any other correspondence!! Why were the papers still in the envelope? What was he hiding from me? Working in medical offices I knew this was highly irregular; the papers should have been available to me.

Luck was with us that day. Dr. Snyder wasn't in the office; they said he was sick. We asked for all my records. You see, in the late seventies no one knew they had the right to just walk into their doctor's office and demand their records. After we asked, they just looked at us with a blank stare, like we were speaking a language they did not understand. We demanded the records, and they finally handed them over.

Lynn and I raced out of there like bats out of hell. Clasping the records for dear life, we drove to a diner and carefully and quickly opened the ENVELOPE. There was a letter from a well-known pharmaceutical company. It urged Dr. Snyder to lower the dose of my medication. They stated that two out of three die of lithium toxicity. Remember I had two lithium toxicities and live to tell the story.

After reviewing my medical records and the contents of the brown envelope, Mr. Goodwin tells me I have a strong case for malpractice. My bladder failure, the neurogenic bladder and the renal tubular acidosis which they found after the first toxic reaction to the lithium, are clear proof of permanent bodily damage. Now the letter from the pharmaceutical company stating that my doctor should reduce the dosage of the medication he is prescribing me for manic depression, which clearly he did not do, will only strengthen my case.

Next, Mr. Goodwin asks me if I know what had happened to Dr. Snyder the week before. I told him I did not, that since moving to Florida I had lost touch with what was going on in the medical community at home. He told me that Dr. Snyder was having chest pains and was rushed to the hospital, suffering from a heart attack. He was released after twenty-four hours; it had been mild.

Two days later, he wasn't feeling well again and called his doctor. The doctor told him to call 9-1-1 and get an ambulance to take him to the hospital. Dr. Snyder said he did not need an ambulance and drove himself to the hospital instead. But on the way, he was hungry and remembered he had not eaten anything that day. He thought lunch might make him feel better. He stopped at a diner on the way and ordered a hamburger and fries. All of sudden he felt very ill again and fainted. They called an ambulance and later Mr. Goodwin found out that Dr. Snyder had suffered a stroke.

We are all taken aback after hearing this story. I believe all things happen for a reason. Mr. Goodwin did not paint a rosy picture about Dr. Snyder's recovery. As a matter of fact, at this point he asks me a very direct question. "Why did I want to file a lawsuit? Was it for revenge or money?" This is an easy question to answer, revenge of course.

Mr. Goodwin expresses his opinion, which is that you do not sue for revenge; you always sue for the money! And in this case his recommendation to me is to go back to Florida and try to live a good life, because it does not look like Dr. Snyder is going to be able to practice medicine any longer and possibly will not live much longer either. Therefore, he isn't going to be able to hurt any more of his patients. But it is my decision to make.

Mr. Goodwin left the room and the three of us, Jack, Lee and I, talk about it. Lee is the one who has been there for most of my problems; he is ten years older than me. And he often encouraged my parents to seek second opinions with other doctors, which they chose not to do. If I want to go forward with the lawsuit, it means returning to the Midwest on a regular basis for depositions prior to the lawsuit going to court.

Mr. Goodwin thinks this kind of case can be held up in the courts for many years, up to ten years. And if Dr. Snyder dies, we will be suing his estate. I decide not to file the lawsuit. I am happy that I have gone through the process and can close this chapter of my life. I will learn to live with the effects of the lithium toxicity, not knowing what is to come, like a walking time bomb.

I thank Mr. Goodwin for his time, and we leave his office. Jack and I are going to stay in the Midwest for a few days to visit with family and friends. I call Susan and ask her if once again she can help me out, because my mother will not let me come over to visit. It is as if my mother is afraid of me.

My mother stood firm. I call her after my meeting with Mr. Goodwin. She says she can't talk and hangs up the phone. That is when I reach out once again to Susan for help. Susan offers her emotional support, as always.

After arriving back at my in-laws' house, there is a message that my mother called asking for me. I immediately call her back. She tells me that Susan has just had a conversation with her. My mother then asks if we can come by the house. That evening Jack and I visit with my parents, and it was good to see them, though things are difficult between my mother and me which I unfortunately am used to.

29

Jack and I fly home to Florida. We both return to work. Michael's glad to hear that I feel I have done all I can about the lawsuit and will not look back and regret not doing it in time. He also has some bad news for me. After I have been the manager of his practice along with the other two doctors in the office for over a year, though the practice is growing, they cannot afford to have a full-time manager any longer. Instead they plan to cover for each other during office hours and hospital rounds.

I understand their predicament, but it means searching for another position. Michael says I can continue working there for the next month, part-time, while I am looking for another job. He provides me with a letter of reference. That day after lunch, I buy a local newspaper and start searching the ads.

That night I go home and tell Jack. I share with him what ads I find and that I will be calling them in the morning. We both agree that a full-time position is best for me to find. The problem is that part-time jobs are all that are available right now.

I check the ads under the medical/dental heading every morning, as we have home delivery of the newspaper to the front door of our condo. It is difficult to find an opening for office management, as most doctors hold on to their managers for years, or an employee that is already in the practice gets a promotion. There are full-time medical positions available for receptionist and insurance clerks.

After looking for a couple of weeks, it starts to become depressing. Depression is not something I have had experience with since my teens. In Florida, I am by myself. I haven't had the opportunity to make friends, and all of my family nearby is new family, Jack's family.

*

The depression becomes debilitating. I do not want to get out of bed in the morning. Jack leaves early for work, usually 7:30

a.m., and does not return home until 6:30 or 7 p.m. He kisses me good-bye and I roll over and stay in bed. And he is not sure how to help me.

I am not eating well either, and exercise is nonexistent. I am listless and lethargic and have no energy or get up and go, and have no interest in intimacy with Jack, though there are other factors that interfere with our intimacy. This isn't like me, and I don't feel comfortable in my own skin. I drag myself out of bed midmorning and look at the paper that Jack left on the kitchen counter for me. It is obvious that finding a new position through the newspaper is not going to happen.

When I was in high school, and had quit working for the cardiologist who pushed his patient too far, I had trouble finding another job. My mother is very resourceful and assertive in some areas of her life. *I wish she had been more so with my health care; maybe I wouldn't have ended up with permanent organ damage.* But nonetheless, she did help me find other positions in medical offices. She would sit down at her desk in the kitchen and open the yellow pages of the phone book to the category for Physicians and call every one of them until she found me a filing/reception position. It was pretty amazing. I had these same traits from her and my father.

As I am moping around my apartment, I am struck by the memory of her ability to stay on task and complete her mission of finding me a job. But she isn't in Florida with me now, and for the most part I am happy about that. It will be difficult for me to grow as an individual if I do not stay out of the Midwest. I know I am not up for the task of finding a job. I do have a phone book, but know that no good can come of me getting on the phone and making calls in the state I am in.

Jack suggests that I get help. I have not seen a psychiatrist since I left the Midwest. And really there is no therapy with Dr. Snyder. He was only there to provide the lithium and review the blood work and the lithium level every three to six months.

I know finding a psychiatrist in Florida does not make sense for the depression as my internist is checking the lithium levels until I make other arrangements. I think finding a therapist will be best. Someone I can talk to who can help me with the depression, not a psychiatrist whose interest is to prescribe medication.

30

I find a therapist, Sheila Post. She isn't much older than I am. In her late twenties or early thirties, she is a psychologist. I hear and now know from experience that it is not always an easy match to find a mental health professional who you click with right away. Sheila is a little stiff, but I am willing to work through it. I feel I don't have a choice, and I hate feeling this desperate.

My first visit with Sheila is difficult. Again, I have no one to lean on, no one to accompany me to the visit, just for moral support, no one at all. She is very clear that from my description of how I am feeling and that getting out of bed in the morning is almost impossible, that I am in a clinical depression. I am not sure what that means. I know that I already have a diagnosis of manic depression, but am ignorant about clinical depression.

Sheila goes on to explain. Clinical depression is a serious mental and medical illness that negatively affects how you feel, the way you think and how you act. Individuals with clinical depression are unable to function normally. Often, they have lost interest in activities that are enjoyable to them, and feel sad and hopeless for long periods of time.

Clinical depression is not the same as feeling sad for a few days and then feeling better. It can affect your body, mood, thoughts and behavior. It can change your eating habits, how you think, your ability to work and study, and how you interact with people. People who suffer from clinical depression often report that they don't feel like themselves anymore and are lost.

It is scary yet reassuring to have Sheila explain exactly what clinical depression is. Scary, because I know that what she is describing to me is exactly what I am feeling, and then reassuring that she is so accurate in her diagnosis. She can see that what she tells me affects me deeply.

She goes on to say that clinical depression is not a sign of personal weakness or a condition that you can wish away. People with clinical depression cannot pull themselves together and get better. In fact, clinical depression often interferes with a person's ability to get help. Fortunately, this is not a problem for me. I realize the first step to getting help is identifying the problem and that I am open to help, but want to form a relationship with trust and comfort, just the way Susan makes me feel.

Next, I ask Sheila what causes clinical depression, even though I think I know the answer. She tells me that I may feel that I know exactly why I am feeling this way. Other times, however, the reasons for depression are not as clear. The causes of depression are quite complex. Very often it is a combination of genetic, psychological and environmental factors. She assures me that regardless of the cause, depression is almost always treatable.

I have been very clear with Sheila and haven't left anything out. She wants to start small, so that it will not be overwhelming. She tells me, does not ask me, that she will be calling me every morning at 8:30 a.m., Monday through Friday to wake me if I am sleeping, and stay on the phone with me until she is sure I am out of bed.

I am ambivalent. First, I do not believe that anyone will do this for me, least of all my new psychologist. Secondly, being held accountable for my behavior and really getting out of bed when she calls seem unrealistic. I share my feelings with Sheila and she insists that this will work for me.

She also wants me to make an appointment with Carl Simpson, MD, who is the head of the practice and able to prescribe medication such as antidepressants. I am not too keen on this idea, since I am already taking lithium. With much persuasion on Sheila's part, I give in and agree to see Dr. Simpson. Sheila arranges the appointment for my convenience, and I will be seeing him later that week.

I leave the office unsure, afraid of being on more medication. I did have a good sense of Sheila's ability and expertise. I realize I have to put my trust in someone, and she is going to be the one for now.

When Jack arrives home after work that evening, I share with him everything about my appointment with Sheila Post, PhD. He says it is a relief that I have gone for help, and that as long as I can put my faith and trust in her treatment plan, he is all for it. It feels like a nice response, yet not very deep, just scratching the surface.

Sheila is true to her word and the next morning the phone rings at 8:30 a.m. Even if I complain about getting out of bed, she is firm and consistent, not only that morning, but on a daily basis for as long as I need it. The plan is for me to see Sheila twice a week.

*

The morning comes for me to meet with Dr. Simpson. He seems young to be so bald. He is no taller than me. I am five foot, seven inches tall. His face is round, abundant eyebrows and adorable dimples; he is soft spoken, yet direct.

Sheila has already spent time reviewing my case with him, so he is somewhat familiar with it. Dr. Simpson, he asks me to call him Carl, suggests adding Prozac to the lithium I am already taking. I am not happy about that. Even though I am not eating well and not overweight, and actually on the skinny side, one hundred and fifteen pounds, thinking about taking a pharmaceutical that has a side effect of adding weight does not please me.

Carl says that it will not be long term and as soon as the majority of the clinical depression passes, he will consider weaning me off the Prozac. Again, having to place my trust somewhere, and after feeling pretty comfortable with Sheila, I decide to take Carl's recommendation and start the Prozac.

Carl explains to me that it can take a month or more to become effective and that I will need to be patient. And there is a chance that it may not help me and that he will have to try a different medication. That all sounds painful. I decide I have no choice.

I stop at the pharmacy and get the prescription on my way home. Carl prescribes the Prozac as follows: one tablet BID, which means one tablet twice a day. It is not a concern about remembering to take it, since I have two pill strips for Monday through Sunday, for my lithium in it already. I just have to add the Prozac.

I do not notice any difference in my depression for a while. It takes at least six weeks until I notice a significant difference. In the meantime, Sheila is still calling me at 8:30 a.m. to make sure I am out of bed. And I continue to have sessions with her twice a week.

They are baby steps. Because I am getting out of bed when Sheila calls and staying out of bed, I am somewhat more productive in my daily life. Not only does Sheila call to be sure I am out of bed, but she spends time asking me what my plans are this morning. She never asks me what I am going to accomplish that day. That would feel overwhelming.

As the weeks go by and I become more and more comfortable with Sheila and her guidance, the black veil starts to lift. I share with Sheila the way my mother suggests searching for jobs. Sheila is very supportive and feels that I am ready to tackle this undertaking. I am not as confident as she is, but together we form a plan.

Each morning after her wake-up call and discussion about how I am going to spend that morning, we decide together that I start with making calls for thirty minutes, being sure to keep a notebook handy to keep track of my conversations and what follow-up will be necessary. Part of me feels afraid, wishing my mother is there to make the calls for me, and part of me does not want to disappoint Sheila, or myself either.

The first week, I accomplish my goal that Sheila and I agree to, but no luck in finding a job. The second week, we decide I will spend more time making calls. It is still a very difficult process, with depression or not. Who will I ask for while making these calls? How am I going to get past the gatekeeper?

If I ask to speak with the office manager, how will that work? It isn't likely that they are about to retire, or are pregnant and leaving their position to raise their baby. But I have trouble thinking of any other approach. Often, after asking the receptionist if I can please speak to the office manager, her response is, I am talking to her. Obviously on these occasions it is a very small medical practice, but working with the yellow pages it is difficult to figure this out before making the calls.

I continue to see Sheila and she encourages me to keep trying, as she says it will only take one practice that needs an office manager with my qualifications. Talk about a needle in a haystack! But with perseverance, I will be successful.

31

It is Thursday morning. I have been searching through the phone book for three weeks now. I call a doctor's office and ask to speak to the office manager. The receptionist says they do not have an office manager at this time, but I can speak to their Healthcare Consultant. Why not? "Sure," I say.

Bill Summer picks up the phone and asks how he can help me. First, he shares with me that he is acting as an interim office manager until they can find one to hire. His role for the practice is a healthcare consultant, which means that he works with the manager and the rest of the staff, in order to streamline systems, appointment scheduling, accounts receivable, hiring and firing the staff, just to name a few of his roles.

I tell him the purpose of my call today is to find a position as a medical office manager. I explain my background and tell him I have a resume and letters of recommendation from my latest employers and the five-doctor practice where I was office manager for two years, along with other positions that I have held in the Midwest before moving to Florida.

Bill asks me how soon I can come to the office for an interview. I do not want to seem overly eager and say now, so instead I tell him I am available the next day in the morning. We schedule the interview for 10 a.m. on Tuesday. There are four doctors in the practice. Bill has been doing medical consulting for over thirty years. He greets me and takes me into Dr. Silver's office, who is the senior partner of the practice. The interview lasts for over an hour. He wants to know all the details about my management skills and finding out what specific things I have done in my other practices. I tell him about my experience hiring and firing staff, training staff, working closely with insurance claims when there is a rejection, and how to work with the insurance companies to insure that the claims are paid.

After the interview Bill shows me around the office and introduces me to all the doctors. He tells them that I am the right candidate for the position and that he wants me to start immediately. I am over the moon! I will be reporting directly to Bill, and I know I am going to enjoy that.

You see, doctors do not get training in medical school regarding business. Most of them are horrible businesspeople. In the past I always have had to report directly to the doctors, and having them comprehend all the details about how each insurance company pays claims is a challenging task at best. Being able to report to Bill will be much easier and more enjoyable; we speak the same language.

I start my new office management position the next morning. I share a large office with three of the billing clerks. It is a welcome change for me. At Michael's office I was there alone most of the day, which sometimes made for very long, slow days, not enough to do. This isn't the case here.

This is a thriving medical practice, among the four doctors they see over eighty patients a day, plus have hospital patients they have to see daily as well. There is an enormous amount of billing and follow-up. Not to mention the current accounts receivables that needs immediate attention.

I now have a purpose. Getting out of bed in the morning is no longer an issue. The depression is gone and I am more myself. I continue to see Sheila Post, but only once every two weeks, instead of twice a week. I discontinue the use of the antidepressants, but do not stop them cold turkey. Carl helps me titrate off the Prozac—go off slowly not cold turkey. I go off the nighttime pill right away for a week, then discontinue the morning dose after that. I continue to take the lithium.

32

Bill is such a nice man; he acts fatherly to me. He knows that I am still a newlywed and that I have not had an opportunity to make many friends. He introduces me to his daughter Audrey; I feel it is an honor. She and I become fast friends, as if we have known each other all our lives. She is so cute and petite and has a bit of a wild side. We always have fun together and most of the time we are laughing.

Audrey has no trouble saying exactly what is on her mind. We are out for dinner one night and for dessert we both order brownie sundaes. The brownies are at the bottom of the bowl, hot and chewy. French vanilla ice cream is on top of the brownies, with hot fudge drizzling down the sides of the ice cream. And walnut pieces everywhere, with whipped cream and a maraschino cherry on top.

Audrey and I both love sugar. Anything with sugar, cakes, cookies, candy and more, but this brownie sundae is especially memorable. While we are devouring the sundaes, Audrey says, "Oh this is orgasmic!" I quickly look around to see if anyone hears her and realize I am the only one and start laughing until I am crying.

We certainly enjoy each other's company and continue to see each other on a regular basis. Then one night when we are walking outside, Audrey tells me all about her recent trip to New York City. Her mother and father are originally from New York and often go back to visit relatives.

Audrey had met Mike at her cousin's house, where she was having dinner. Mike is friends with her cousin Jimmy. Audrey is so happy; she says he is tall and hot, dark brown hair and dark green eyes that smile all the time, and especially when he is talking to her. They walk in Central Park and visit the museums. They hit it off instantly. That is no surprise to me. Audrey says that she has been happy growing up in Florida, but would like to try living in the north, and that Mike is going to ultimately give her that opportunity.

Mike and Audrey speak every day by phone and see each other at least twice a month. It is a whirlwind romance, and they announce their engagement after only dating five months. They are so in love they do not want to be away from each other; they set the date for their wedding.

I am so happy for Audrey and so sad for myself. I have finally made a friend, a great friend. I am hoping it will not set me back emotionally, since my relationship with Jack is not as close as it once was, and I have not made any other friends yet.

*

Audrey and her father Bill are both very creative and make the place cards and centerpieces for the wedding. Audrey is a beautiful bride. She looks like a princess and Mike looks like her prince. The ceremony is beautiful, and the reception is fun as well. Audrey and I cling to one another when we say good-bye, and promise each other to stay in touch. And Audrey will come back home to visit too.

33

Jack and I are going through the motions in our marriage. There really are not many sparks. It is just like a boring train ride, watching the countryside go by, and it all looks the same. I realize that I need to ask Sheila to help me with my relationship with Jack. Now that the depression is gone, there is more to fix.

I see Sheila a couple of days later. She has some news for me. She is pregnant and will be leaving her practice. She does not plan to return to work after the baby is born. I am very happy for her, but again sad for myself. I have just lost Audrey. I have a certain comfort level with Sheila. What is going to happen now?

Sheila suggests that I see Carl for therapy. It is 1981, and psychiatrists are still doing therapy. I miss Sheila at first, then become comfortable with Carl. I realize it is easier for me to talk to a man. Maybe it has something to do with growing up in a home with four men. Or that I do not feel comfortable or confident in most of the advice my mother gives me.

I talk to Carl about my marriage and how uncomfortable I am; more to the point, how I find myself lonely even with Jack in the room. I realize there is something very wrong with this. Carl suggests that Jack and I schedule some time alone, quality time to be with one another.

I take Carl's advice. Since it is Friday, I decide to ask Jack if he wants to go for a ride on Saturday, possibly to Key Largo, about an hour from home. Jack thinks it is a great idea and we take off early Saturday in his Volkswagen Rabbit, with the sunroof open and the stereo blasting.

We often go to the Florida Keys to visit his family. His cousins Molly and Paul own a house in Islamorada, about halfway down the Keys. The private beaches there are exquisite. When the tide is going out, you can walk in the shallow waters. There are sandbars that are so large you can lay down in the middle of the water on one and watch the clouds go by; a little slice of heaven.

It is March 6, 1982, to be exact. We are off to Key Largo and the news comes on the radio that John Belushi is dead. This is shocking news; we love John Belushi and *Saturday Night Live*. The news report says the cause of his death is a speedball, a combination injection of cocaine and heroin. It is unclear at the time if it is an accident or not. Later the reports call it an accident.

We drive quietly to Key Largo, neither of us feeling like conversing. About thirty minutes into our ride, Boston comes on the radio. Boston is Jack's favorite group; we try to enjoy the rest of the ride.

*

We have been looking for a house to buy and I am spending early evenings before Jack gets home from work, meeting our real estate agent at homes for sale. His name is George Newman. He is mainly showing me one-story houses with one-car garages and no basements. In Florida there are no basements, as it is too close to sea level.

I look at about twenty houses with George and pick three that I like most. That is when I ask Jack to take a tour of the homes on a Saturday morning. It is a quick decision for him as to which house he likes best. Jack is looking for a house that is going to make his commute to work easiest.

We put a bid in on the house. It is a cute house. The front of the house is reclaimed brick, brick that has been repurposed from demolition sites. The edges of the brick are typically worn and irregular. The bricks are many different colors, which gives them a charm and character of their own. The front door is brick red and the garage door is white, which matches the trim around the windows of the house. There is a bay window to the left of the front door, where the living room is.

One thing that is hard to understand is that the front door of the houses in Florida swing out when you open them. I ask George why all the houses are built like that. He explains that in Florida, the doors of the houses have to open outward because of the building code. It is to help protect from hurricane-force winds blowing the doors in.

This makes me think about houses at home. I ask my brother Lee why doors in our houses in the Midwest open inward. And he tells me the reason for doors opening inward up north is also a building code. It is so you can dig out when there is a snowstorm and the snow piles up against the front door.

All the furniture from our condo fits nicely in our new home. The only things we need to buy are a bed for the guest room and a couch for the den. We even have furniture for the patio.

Packing and unpacking boxes is something that is not a chore for me. Within two weeks we are totally done unpacking. Even though we have only been married for two years, we seem to have too many things that we really do not want or need. I suggest we have a garage sale. Jack likes the idea. As I unpack, I accumulate things that I want to get rid of in the garage sale. Jack spends some time going through his things as well.

The garage sale is going to be Saturday morning from 7 a.m. to 10 a.m. Jack makes the signs and posts them in the neighborhood. I plan on preparing the items when I get home from work on Friday.

That evening, I move the patio table to the driveway and then open the garage to bring the aluminum table out to the driveway as well. Being that the garage door is not electric, I push it open as far as it goes, but it really needs repair.

I am walking back and forth in and out of the garage when the garage door slips closed. It closes on me my head to be exact. I am able to reach up and shove it open. I go inside the house and sit down. I don't feel well—nauseous and fuzzy in my head. I decide to put my head between my legs so I do not faint. It helps a little bit, and I get a glass of water and decide to lie down for a while.

Jack wakes me when he gets home from work. I am not sure how long I have been sleeping. I tell Jack about the accident, and he wonders if I have a concussion. Being alone when the garage door fell on my head, I really am not sure.

Jack puts a frozen pizza in the oven for dinner and we go to sleep early, as we have to get up early for the garage sale. The next morning it is raining, and no one shows up. Fortunately, the only things that get wet are the tables. I haven't had an opportunity to put our things out on them. We decide to leave all the things in the boxes and donate them to Goodwill.

Things are not going well between Jack and me. I thought moving into our own home might help give us more privacy, and just plain pride in owning our first home together. It doesn't matter. Jack still comes home from work each night and gives me a kiss on the cheek and walks right into our bedroom to change into a tee shirt and cutoffs. I have dinner ready, we eat together talking about our day, and right after dinner he rolls a joint and starts smoking. I am allergic to smoke. He really doesn't care. He opens the window in the den, to appease me. I always worry that the neighbors might smell the marijuana and call the police.

I go into our bedroom and put a towel on the floor next to the bottom of the door, to keep the smoke out. I read or call a friend back home and then fall asleep, by myself. I really do not know when Jack comes to bed. He never complains about the towel by the door, so I guess he can open it without too much effort. From my therapy with Sheila and Carl, I know that unless we connect, meaning we have some kind of intimacy in our marriage, our marriage is in deep trouble.

*

The highlight of my day is going to work. Bill Summer is a true mentor. He teaches me to go beyond medical office management, into the consulting world. Bill tells me I am ready to do medical consulting, a step up from management. I learn more in-depth accounting techniques from him, along with the ability to connect with the doctors and employees, knowing that there is a window of time to complete a job, and then move forward to the next client, or work part-time for many clients at the same time.

I understand the importance of the working relationship I have with Bill. He has faith in my expertise and passion for getting the job done. And if I have questions about an issue it is OK to say to the client that I do not have an answer, but will get one. This is a new concept for me, as I think I always have to have an answer right away in order to be successful.

*

It becomes clear to me that if my marriage to Jack is not going to survive, I will be able to support myself. That I can move forward alone and be productive and make it on my own. After all, I already feel alone when Jack is in the room with me. A sad state of events.

34

As my relationship with Jack keeps creeping downward, I know I have to do more to try to save it. I believe that all the therapy in the world isn't going to help. Relationships take a lot of work, but it takes two. I cannot fix it alone. I speak with Jack on numerous occasions, and he tells me he is happy the way things are. But he says he has an idea that will spice things up.

Before he is ready to share his idea with me; he tells me he realizes that prior to our marriage when we would go away for the weekend once a month, part of his motivation for that was to stick it to his mother. In other words, he knew she did not approve of us having sex prior to being married. Her constant reminders of this were an annoyance to him. Once we were married, the annoyance went away, and sex was no longer a tool he could use against his mother.

Jack tells me his idea to spice of our relationship. I can't even write about it, that is how unacceptable it is. I know I have to get out. I tell Jack that I am going to move into my parents' house for a while. I need to sort things out by myself.

The house is empty, because my parents are still living in the Midwest at the time. They are snowbirds, flying to Florida during the wintertime. I pack a small bag of things I need for the next few days and tell Jack I will come back for more of my things when he is at work.

I stop at the grocery store on the way to my parents' house to fill up the fridge. I also call them and tell them that things are not working out and I need a safe place to stay. They say OK, but I can tell they aren't happy about it. I am not sure if they are unhappy about my relationship with Jack beginning to fail or that I am staying in their house. It is unclear.

Life goes on and I go through the motions. I work Monday through Friday and am not sure what I am going to do on the weekend. But I never make it to the weekend. My parents and Jack are in constant communication, as it turns out. My parents quiz Jack about my moods. They insist that I must be having a manic episode and he needs to take charge and get me into a hospital, a psychiatric hospital, and if I don't go willingly he needs to commit me to a state institution. Jack has no backbone and no faith in me, or he would fight this.

During the time at my parents' house I have been talking with my friend Kevin. I had met my friend Carol in a cooking class I took, and she introduced me to her husband Kevin. Kevin and I have a lot in common. We both love interior design and cooking, and we often get together. Kevin and I become best friends. Jack and Carol are not too happy about it either.

There is nothing sexual between us; we are platonic friends who have a deep connection. We understand each other to the core. Carol and Kevin have two small children, a boy and a girl. Things have not been good between them for a long time, prior to me and Jack meeting them.

Kevin and Carol separate and soon after, get a divorce. Kevin is a great dad and shares custody of the kids. Kevin built a custom home for his family, so Carol decides to move out and find a small house for her and the kids.

Kevin is totally supportive and encourages me to think things through carefully, because Jack and I have been together for over eight years and maybe we can get past Jack's insane idea and even grow from the experience.

Even though Kevin and I are very close, he does not know that I suffer from manic-depressive illness. I do not have a choice now. My parents, especially my mother, are trying to convince Jack that I am indeed having a manic episode and that he needs to get me out of their house and into the psych ward as soon as possible.

*

Jack does not have a key to my parents' house. He has come by twice, first ringing the doorbell and then pounding on the door to let him in. I have all the blinds down in the house and lie down on the bed with a pillow over my head, praying that he leaves.

When he finally does, I call Kevin. He comes over to visit me. I tell him about my illness and how my parents have kept it in the closet, and I feel that is where I belong too. I do not share my diagnosis with anyone. Not even doctors.

Kevin is not a judgmental person and says that plenty of people have mental illness. And no one needs to know about it. I tell him about my mother, who is pushing Jack, trying to convince him I am having a manic episode and that he has to admit me to a psychiatric hospital or commit me to a state institution. He stops cold and looks me right in the eye and says, "That's ridiculous."

Kevin says I seem as clear-headed as ever, and that finding out what Jack is asking of me, things that are not normal and surely not safe, is probably the best thing that can happen. Especially if we haven't had any children yet, this is a time of reflection for me perhaps I need to take my life in another direction—away from Jack and my mother.

It feels as though it is just a matter of time before my mother wears Jack down and forces me to sign myself into the psych ward. I am furious about the whole thing. I already feel like an animal in a cage. Jack should be defending me. He knows what I had been though as a teenager.

My intuition is on red alert. I know I am not going to be able to stay at my parents' house and find any peace. I feel that my mother will convince Jack to commit me to a place where I do not belong, with drug addicts, alcoholics, schizophrenics and people who are suicidal.

The next day, Jack comes to their house. He is relentless; he will not leave and keeps banging on the door. I want to call the police, but think that will make the situation worse, and thinking of leaving my parents' house in a straitjacket is too horrifying and not an option.

Instead, I finally break down and open the door. He marches in, which is something different for him to be so assertive. He sits me down and tells me I have no other option but to sign myself into the psychiatric ward today. If I don't, my mother has told him she will help him get me committed. Again, the thought of a straitjacket and being in a snake pit are front and center in my mind. What if that means a state institution instead of a private psychiatric ward? I can be there for months. I have heard too many true stories about people who have been taken away to a state institution, and it seems that the minimum stay is six months.

I am shaking with every fiber of my being. Not again. I am an adult, why can't I get some kind of respect, or at least have Jack treat me like a person, a human being? It is too scary to even cry, and let down my defenses. I tell Jack that I will go, but not with him.

I have not given my psychiatrist Carl a call yet. I am afraid. I feel if I call him that Jack and my mother will somehow turn Carl against me. So instead, judgment day has come, and I am going to have to sign myself in to the hospital that my mother picks. She finds a psychiatrist near Key Biscayne by the name of Joe Ross, MD. On my mother's recommendation I will have to sign myself into the hospital where he has privileges.

I know that trying to talk to anyone in my family will not help. Not even Susan can reach my mother when she is on the warpath. I do speak with Susan, and she is angry and finds it disappointing that my mother does not stay out of my life and let me make my own decisions. Susan wonders how my mother can be making this ludicrous decision to put me in a psych unit again. After all, my mother is hundreds of miles away. How can she really know what is going on? It feels like she is trying to destroy me all over again!

I tell Jack to get out. I will be at the psych hospital at 2 p.m. The first thing I do after Jack leaves is bolt the front door and call Kevin. I start to ask him if he will take me to the hospital. But at this point I am sobbing uncontrollably, and he can't understand a word I am saying. After finally calming down a bit, between sobs I ask him again if he will come to my parents' house and take me to the psych ward. He says he is on his way over.

Kevin sits with me for a while and brings me something to eat. He knows I am having trouble eating and sleeping. And that is a perfect formula for becoming manic. I am physically and emotionally a wreck from this whole unnecessary ordeal that my mother is putting me through again. Jack is just a weakling going along with her. My mother may not have control over me the way she did when I was younger, but she obviously can control Jack and is doing just that. I have no self-worth and nowhere to go. I can't go back to Michigan; no one there will help me. And I am not confident enough to get in my car and drive to a hotel and stay alone there, as my PTSD from the hallucinations during the lithium toxicity starts again. What other choices are there?

Kevin drives me to the hospital and sits in the waiting area with me. He takes my hand and encourages me to be the strong person that he knows I am. He tells me that I have to make a game out of this. He feels strongly that my mother and Jack are the ones out of control. He says that I am in a bad marriage, with bad parents who will not let me live my life nor give me credit for being the capable adult that I have become.

His words are very reassuring. But I know it went deeper than his words. We love each other as best friends, and we help and protect one another and certainly have each other's back. Kevin's words become a mantra for me. I repeat them over and over, remembering that he has total faith in my sanity.

He suggests if I have access to a phone, to call him every day and he will continue to support me. While we are sitting in the waiting area, a receptionist comes over to me and hands me a clipboard with papers on it. They are the papers that I have to sign in order to enter the psychiatric ward. I am an adult in the eyes of the law, 25 years old, but am not an adult in the eyes of my family, especially my mother and my husband. Therefore, I have to sign the papers voluntarily, or my other option is to have the men in the white coats take me away to the state institution. Jack will commit me. And if I do not cooperate, that's exactly what he will do.

Finally it is time to go, once again behind doors that lock from the outside, with windows that have bars on them. I have to surrender myself, as if I am going to jail for a crime I did not commit. Walking through the doorway and hearing the heavy door close and knowing that if I turn around and try to push the door open it will not give, not one inch, it is torture. I am lost. Spinning and spinning I have no control of my life once again. I feel broken, but must stand tall.

*

The orderly takes me into a room, a stark room, that has dirty white walls, two beds, one nightstand, a barren-looking dresser and a small window with bars on it. He tells me to sit on the bed and wait for the nurse. Empty, alone, total despair are just a few words to describe how I feel. I am numb, tears run down my face.

I have lost track of time. I don't know how long it takes for the nurse to come into the room. But I know the drill. She looks through my suitcase to make sure I don't have anything dangerous in there, anything that I can hurt myself with, like a belt to hang myself. I do not want to kill myself. I am not suicidal. Why am I here in the first place?

Slowly the minutes turn into hours. The nurse gives me a tour of the floor. It is one big rectangle. With doors for the inmates' rooms, I mean patients' rooms, bathrooms with signs Men and Women on the doors, the bathrooms have shower stalls in them too. A nursing station, where every nurse looks like Nurse Ratched, and there is a common room where patients sit, have meals and watch TV, but most of them are in a haze, shuffling from place to place unable to lift their feet off the floor properly. It is the Thorazine shuffle. Thorazine is an antipsychotic drug, to treat people who are experiencing psychosis, meaning having hallucinations or delusions. Unfortunately, I am familiar with this. I have seen it before. To the best of my knowledge, I have absolutely no recollection of being given this drug that turns you into a robot.

The rest of the tour is uneventful, until the nurse gets to the very end of the hall and I see open doors to rooms with nothing in them except a bare mattress on the floor. There are four rooms that all look exactly the same. I don't need an explanation of what the rooms are for. They are seclusion rooms. Like the one I had been put in almost ten years before, for rearranging my room in the psych ward in the Midwest. The one where my parents left me there for extra days, when they had to go out of town, you know like daycare, but it really was a hell hole.

I am going to be on my best behavior. I am not going to end up in one of these rooms, not ever. Sadly, I am wrong.

*

I sign myself into the psych ward on Saturday. Sunday, I get up and put my clothes on and go to the common room for breakfast. After breakfast I decide to go back to my room and get in my robe and take a shower.

I am not familiar with the staff. Actually, I want to keep it that way. There are staff people there that I did not see the day before. Keep in mind I am 25 years old, five foot, seven, one hundred and twenty pounds, with blonde hair and blue eyes.

Right after breakfast I need to walk by the nursing station to return to my room. There is a guy standing there leaning against the counter. I don't think he is a nurse. I guess he is an orderly. He is over six feet tall, built like a football player. I walk by him trying not to have eye contact, and he calls out to me, not by name. I look around to see who he is talking to and realize I am the only one in the hallway. So I have to acknowledge him. I look up at him.

There is no one else at the nursing station at the time. He continues to glare at me and says, "Hey babe, you are new here, aren't you?" I say yes and that I am not his babe, and I continue to walk down the hall. Talking to him at all is a mistake, even though I speak evenly and directly to him.

I go back to my room to get ready for my shower. I gather my shampoo, soap etc., and off I go down the hall to the women's bathroom. There are four toilet stalls, four sinks and four showers in the bathroom. Nothing fancy of course, hospital drab. There is no one in the bathroom but me. The showers are in a square shape. Two showers on the left side and two showers on the right side; I choose the one on the left side closest to the corner of the room. I put my things down on the stool along with a towel that I take out of a bin by the sinks.

I walk over to the shower and reach in to turn the water on. When the temperature is right, I remove my robe and place it on the stool. I enter the shower and close the beige curtain. I get my hair wet and reach out to the stool for my shampoo. I squeeze shampoo into my hand and place the bottle back on the stool. I start to work the shampoo into my hair. And then it happens. Out of nowhere, the male orderly abruptly, with no notice, pulls back the shower curtain. I immediately grab the towel from the stool and hold it up to the front of my body. He literally picks me up and carries me over his shoulder down the hall. I am struggling to get away from him. Surprisingly, I am not kicking and screaming like one might have thought; I am using all my might to get away from him.

This is impossible. I know where he is taking me. I am frantic, I am crying, the tears streaming down my face, hard to distinguish from the rest of me. Cold, wet, shampoo in my hair, nude except for the towel that is covering the front of my body. It is such a blur, but it is not just me and this brute of a man, this wild animal who stands on two feet carrying me down the hall. There are people watching, staring and not helping me in anyway.

He throws me onto the mattress, laughing and telling me no one messes with him. He stands there and stares at me as I am clenching the towel to my body, teeth chattering. Then he abruptly leaves the room, the seclusion room, but not without closing the huge metal door, locking it from the outside.

At this point I stop crying. I am furious and still soaking wet. I wrap the towel around my body. After all, it is not a fluffy large towel like I have a home, it is a thin small old threadbare towel, and it has lost its bold white color years ago and barely covers me. The mattress is bare, no sheet. Because if there is a sheet someone might rip it up and tie it together and try to hang themselves from the bars on the window. The window is high above my head. I can't even reach it standing on the mattress.

So there I am alone again, in a world that makes no sense to me. Kneeling on this barren, dirty-looking and disgusting mattress; I decide to move to the floor, but after a while it is too hard to kneel on. I try to gather myself. I look around this desolate room. Four dirty white walls, one small window high on the wall, with bars on it, and a large heavy door with a small window, with metal running horizontally and vertically through the middle of the glass. Then I see it in the corner of the room, the corner near the large door, a camera able to look right at the mattress, right at me.

This is horrifying once again. I should have known, but how could I know? They are watching me. This time they are watching me, other times they are watching whoever else is in seclusion. I start to pray. I have such a strong belief in God. Without Susan and God how could I have survived this long? Each and every time climbing out of the hellhole I am in, finding the strength to go on. I can get through this. I have to so I can strangle Jack when I get out of here.

Five days and nights pass and the doctor in charge of me, Joe Ross, MD, decides I am ready to go home. I tell him that the first time I meet him. He doesn't listen and does not care.

Both my mother and Jack had made sure I was at a hospital that Carl wasn't on staff at. They will not admit it when I approach them about it; but it has to be true. I think that Carl would have asked me to come to his office for a visit and not agree with the way Jack was handling the situation. Though in all the commotion, that is not the way it went down.

*

When I get home from the pysch ward, it is hard for me to understand how I can continue to stay with Jack. Even after what he has done to me, I stay. The last few months I have felt like I was drowning in quicksand, and there is still such a lack of communication and respect. I wonder if I am some kind of an addict, similar to how an alcoholic, drug or gambling addict feels. They just keep going back for more, even when deep down, very deep down, they know it isn't good for them.

35

Weeks then months go by, and nothing much changes between Jack and me. We both work all day and sometimes have dinner together and still never go to sleep at the same time. After a while I feel hopeless, alone and l have no marriage at all.

It is spring. If you live in Florida long enough you do notice the change in seasons, of course not as noticeable as in the north. The trees do start to bloom, and the flowers start to grow. And the allergy season starts.

I start taking Sudafed for my allergies and like the way it works. After several weeks of taking it I realize I am getting shaky and having trouble sleeping. I go for an office visit to my internist. He does not like the way I look and tells me I am dehydrated as well. He wants to admit me to the hospital.

Again, this is pretty standard for the early eighties. Admit the patient for a work-up and the admitting physician can bill the insurance company for the three to four days you are in the hospital.

My internist calls my endocrinologist for a consultation. When James Burn, MD, my endocrinologist, comes to see me, he and my internist are having a difference of opinion. Dr. Burn wants me to stay on my thyroid medication and my internist does not. Instead, he wants to take me off the Sudafed and thyroid medicine and start from scratch. Dr. Burn insists that is the wrong approach and will put me at risk. It will take weeks to regulate my thyroid again if I stop taking the medicine.

I am an adult, even if my husband and parents do not treat me like one. I know Dr. Burn is making the right decision by keeping me on my thyroid medication. I certainly have not forgotten when I was first diagnosed as a teenager and had been given steroids, and how terrible that turned out. And then how my thyroid disease had been under control as soon as Dr. Howard started me on thyroid replacement.

The first night I am in the hospital Jack visits me. He comes into my room with his tail between his legs and sits down on the large chair next to the hospital bed. He says he has something to tell me. He wants me to know that he will never stop loving me. But his mother tells him I will always be sick, and he is leaving me. She says I am "Damaged Merchandise"!

I begin to cry, and he says he is sorry and leaves. I call my brother Warren and tell him Jack has just left me. He tells me that he is going to fly to Florida and have a few words with my husband. I ask him not to come, and make him promise not to tell mom and dad. He says OK for now, but plans on telling our other two brothers. I agree to that.

A couple days later I go home from the hospital. Jack takes all his clothes and moves out. I have been in touch with my parents, and as it turns out Warren does not keep his promise and tells my parents that Jack has left me. So much for that.

I am furious with Jack that he never had a backbone; as a matter of fact he is a mama's boy. It is still hard for me to believe that he walked out on me when I was in the hospital. He is a coward. But it is kinder in the end; he does me a favor.

However, I do not see it that way yet. We have been together for eight years and I am going to fight to get him back. That is just what I do. I call him often, go to his office, which is almost an hour by car from home, and try to think of any other ways to get his attention, just short of stalking him. I pursue him for almost six months and then realize it is over for good and I need to move on. I start dating. I go to happy hour after work and make some new friends.

36

Several months later, I am in-between clients, and while I am looking for a new one, I take a part-time job at Bloomingdale's. I am the perfume person, the one who greets you before or after you get off the escalator, wanting to know if you want to try the new fragrance the store is offering. It is there that I meet my lifelong friend Maggie Levon. She is working in the crystal and china department, while looking for a teaching job. Interesting how we are both working there temporarily and happen to meet.

After working for two short weeks I find a new client. It is a group of five gastroenterologists that own an office condominium. They decide they no longer want to be partners, and they split up their practice, but continue to share space. Two doctors hire me, Richard Leaf, MD, and Ralph Holmes, MD, to manage and hire their new staff. They ask me to stay for a six- month period.

These two doctors have similar professional styles, yet are very different in all other ways. Richard Leaf is newly single and looking for a girlfriend. He invites the whole staff to his house for lunch, and one time he shows us the movie *Purple Rain* with Prince. Ralph Holmes is a family man with two small children, and a lovely wife and home. He invites all of us to his house for a bar-be-que–swim party. He indeed has a beautiful family, something I aspire to.

I hire Maureen Wilson, a young girl just out of high school, as a file clerk. She proves to be a valuable employee and wants to learn more about working in a medical office. I take Maureen under my wing. Her mother passed away a couple of years ago and her father is remarried and already has a baby or two. Maureen feels out of place at home and needs nurturing. That is where I come in.

Dr. Holmes' nurse Gloria does the filing. She is always behind, having to take care of patients most of the time. When Maureen starts doing the filing, it is done quickly and she has extra time in her day to help me. I teach her how to post insurance payments; she is a natural, very good with numbers and details.

After the six-month mark, Dr. Leaf asks me to sit down in his office with him. He tells me how happy he is with how the management and finances of the practice are going. He wants me to stay for another three months. During the same meeting he tells me why Dr. Holmes has not been in the office the last two days.

He reveals to me that Dr. Holmes took an overdose of prescription medicine on purpose, in my office. Dr. Leaf says that he came in my office and found Dr. Holmes unconscious three nights ago. I am taken aback. Appearances from the outside seem that Dr. Holmes is a happy man. But appearances are just that, appearances.

Dr. Holmes is going to be fine. Dr. Leaf finds him in time to save his life. After hearing this story, I feel it is a signal for me to move on. I have done my job here and do not want to work in an office all day where someone tried to kill himself.

That is when I find the position at Ned Yearly, MD's office. I take Maureen with me. She drives to my condo every morning and we drive together to Ned's office. The arrangement works out well.

Soon after moving on from Drs. Leaf and Holmes' practice, I hear that Dr. Holmes filed for divorce. And soon after that he asked his nurse Gloria to marry him. I always wondered why she was in his office for such a long time every day when he came back from doing his rounds at the hospital. Now I know. It is a real soap opera.

*

It is now a year since I had the bladder failure. Life goes on and I have a checkup with Dr. Smyth. He tells me that my bladder is strong enough to support a baby, and that I am free to try to get pregnant. I tell him that my husband has left me and that getting pregnant is not a priority at the moment. But I am glad that after taking medication for over a year, my bladder muscle is strong enough to support a baby.

There is a knock at the door that evening. It is a sheriff; serving me with divorce papers. The sheriff is a big man; he blocks the sun when I open the door. I had asked Jack to have his divorce attorney serve my divorce attorney, but obviously that did not happen.

The next morning, I call my attorney, James Green. I tell him about the sheriff and being served with the divorce papers. He is sorry to hear this. He asks me to drop off the papers at his office. James says that I do not have to appear in front of the judge during the final divorce proceedings if I don't want to. After some thought, I decide I want to, for closure.

I have to appear in court the following week, on Thursday to be exact. The night before the court appearance, I hear the front door open. I always come in through the garage and hardly ever open my front door. It is Jack. He uses his key and walks right in the house. He says he has made a terrible mistake and wants to come back to me. He says he will call his attorney early in the morning to cancel the hearing.

I am in shock and angry all at the same time. This is surreal. Jack letting himself into, yes, it is still our house, but he has not been living with me for over six months. I finally am moving on. I now have the confidence and know I can live alone and find someone else to be with who is mature and their own person, and build a future with him. I take a deep breath and show Jack to the door. I contact a locksmith in the morning.

The next morning I go to the courthouse and meet James there. We walk into the courthouse together. James tells me that the hearing is going to take place on the second floor in a conference room, where Jack's attorney, the judge and the court reporter will be.

The judge comes into the room and sits at the head of the table. I am sitting next to James on one side of the table and Jack is sitting with his attorney on the other side of the table. Jack does not have any eye contact with me. No surprise after last night's attempt to get me back.

It is a short hearing. The judge asks a couple of questions. I know they are standard questions for a divorce, but they still feel intrusive. He asks me directly if I am pregnant. I find this offensive and laughable, considering everything I have been through. James looks at me after hesitating a moment. I say I am not pregnant.

37

I decide to join a dating service and I meet Mike Fox. We talk on the phone for over an hour when he calls to ask me out. The next day I receive one dozen yellow roses from Mike. It is very sweet of him. That evening he takes me out to dinner.

Mike and I meet at the restaurant. It is about halfway between the two cities we live in. I do not feel comfortable having someone I do not know come to my home and pick me up, roses or not.

Mike is originally from New Jersey. His home is over half an hour from my place. We have a wonderful time at dinner. Mike is tall and good looking; he works for a national insurance company. He asks me out for the weekend, and I accept.

Mike and I are exclusive for a while. He lives fifteen minutes from my client; and it is easy for me to go to Mike's for dinner after work. He is an excellent cook. Mike and I date for another couple of months and then we go our separate ways. He isn't very affectionate, and I need affection in my life.

I do not want to revisit the dating service right now. So, instead, the local newspaper has a new personals section in their Sunday magazine. Why not, I think. I will put an ad in. Not wanting to provide my phone number, I use the service that the newspaper offers; so the men who want to respond to my ad can write to a PO Box that the newspaper provides and they then forward the letters to me.

This is what the ad says: "SWF, blonde hair, blue eyes, tall and thin. I enjoy travel, the arts and sports, looking for SWM who has similar interests." I receive thirty-three responses. It is a lot of fun sitting and reading the letters. Two are from men in prison who are looking for a wife. I throw those letters out. There is one from a man who lives about an hour by car from my condo. It seems to me that this is a good place to start. If he has an interest in meeting me after we speak on the phone and is willing to drive the distance to meet me, he is probably worth it.

We have a great conversation on the phone, and he offers to take me to dinner. I think it best to meet at a restaurant the first time. We both like Cuban food, so we meet at a local place near my home.

*

During this time, I put our house up for sale. I call George Newman who I have become friends with since buying our house and ask him to list it for us. In the meantime, I want to stay in the area and have found two condos I like. They are both being built at the same time.

One is a two-bedroom and one-bath unit. The other is a one-bedroom, one-bath. It has European cabinetry in the kitchen, so that is the one I pick. Another reason I choose it is because I don't really want a two-bedroom unit. It makes me feel like I have to have a roommate. Something I am not ready for. I need to find peace living alone.

I watch my condo being built. Kevin often comes with me to see the progress of the construction. He is very helpful, and I appreciate his friendship. It is a garden-style condo, on the first floor of a four-story building. When you walk in, on the left is a closet door that has a stackable washer and dryer behind it, along with storage space. To the right is a door that leads to the bathroom. Straight ahead is the living room, which has a large glass sliding door. There is a patio outside along with a storage room. Next to the living room is a dining room and behind that is the kitchen. The bedroom is large enough for a king-size bed. The bedroom is off the living room and has a large walk-in closet. There is a door to the bathroom from the master bedroom as well. It is just enough room for me. I love it.

*

Sam Camel is the name of the man who lives an hour away. We meet for dinner and he gives me a large basket of flowers. They are beautiful, flowers of rainbow colors. The basket is so large I place it in the back seat of my car while we are having dinner. I know that Sam is newly single and shares custody with his ex-wife of their two young boys, who are five and seven.

This is something I think of often. I really do not plan on being a stepmother. My goal is to marry again and have children. I believe it is like anything else in life, the more men I meet, the better chance I have finding the right one.

Dinner is delicious, chicken and rice, black beans and plantains, and flan for dessert. I really enjoy Cuban cuisine. Being with Sam is fun. He is easygoing and mature; he is seven years older than me and is part of a successful family business. He seems to have all the time in the world to relax and enjoy life.

After a couple of dates, Sam and I begin seeing each other every week. He often comes to my place, and once a month I drive to his place and spend the weekend with him. He knows that I have a Club Fun trip coming up and urges me to cancel it. He says he has heard bad things about women traveling alone to these resorts; he just doesn't want me to go.

Prior to meeting Sam, my friend Beth suggested I take a trip to get away from it all. She has just come back from a Club Fun trip to Turks and Caicos. The trip is all-inclusive meals, accommodations and flight. It sounds great to me. It is a short plane ride and I need the break. I book the trip and off I go.

I fly to Turks and Caicos on a Saturday. I arrive on the island midmorning, and after clearing customs, take a shuttle to the resort. There are many small buildings that have four rooms in each. I have a room that is near the beach on the second floor. My friend Beth did not share with me that there are no room keys, as there are no locks on the door. It is1985.

I quickly unpack and get into a bikini to join a group of people who are going snorkeling. We are all standing around on the dock. It is a beautiful spring day, with a temperature around seventy-five degrees and a light breeze in the air. The snorkel instructor, Juan, is from the island itself. He asks us to pick partners. I am the only one left without a partner, so Juan offers to be my partner.

Yes, this is my lucky day. I certainly can have a great time knowing that I have the instructor as my partner. We all put on our snorkel gear, mask, fins, etc. and jump off the side of the boat into the water. It is a fun afternoon; the waters are very clear and you can see all the sea creatures, schools of fish, starfish, crabs, sea rays, turtles and more.

After the lesson, I return to my room to shower and change for dinner. I meet a lot of nice people, including Cheryl, a woman from Colorado. We both have come alone to the resort, and since we hit it off, we decide to spend time together. We have meals and sun on the beach together often.

One night after dinner, Cheryl and I go for a walk on the sand and hear music coming from a gazebo at the end of the beach. We check it out and end up sitting down and listening to the music. It is typical island music, and we order a drink. Juan the snorkel instructor comes over to say hello to me. I think nothing of it at the time.

When Cheryl and I are ready to return to our rooms, Juan says he will walk us there. We both say no thanks and leave. Our rooms are not close to one another, so we say good-bye after walking back up the beach together.

The next morning after breakfast, Cheryl and I go to the beach together. I am wearing a white bikini and Cheryl has a black one on. We order some juice from the waiter who walks up and down the beach to serve the guests. It is a quiet, peaceful morning.

Cheryl and I decide to meet for lunch after we both go back to our rooms to shower and change. As I am walking back to my room, Juan comes out of nowhere. He asks me if I am going to meet him later in the day to go snorkeling. I tell him no.

I am starting to have a bad feeling about Juan. I go up to my room and instinctively want to lock the door, and then remember, no locks. I take my empty suitcase and place it up against the door and quickly shower. I am glad to see that the suitcase is in the same place I left it before my shower.

I tell Cheryl about Juan and she says she will be sure to stay close to me during the rest of the week. That evening when Cheryl walks me to my room and I thank her, something does not feel right. I turn and there is Juan coming up the sand in the direction of my room. He asks me if I want to have a drink with him. I tell him no and start walking toward an area where people are gathering. I know going into my room is not an option at this point. Even if I try to block the doorway, Juan will be able to get into my room.

He is walking very close to me. I start to run, but it is too late. Juan grabs me by the arm and throws me down on the ground. I may be five foot, seven, but only weigh one hundred and seventeen pounds. Fortunately, Juan is barely my height, but still is certainly stronger than me. I struggle to get away from him and then decide to appear calm and knee him in the crotch and run away as fast as I can.

I find an employee of Club Fun and tell him about Juan. He placates me and keeps saying that Juan is harmless, just an island boy. I tell him I want to call the police. There is only one pay phone in the resort; no phones in the rooms. He says he will call the police for me after he walks me to my room to be sure I am OK and feeling better.

Calm down, feeling better, not quite! I want nothing more than to pack my things and get the next plane out of there. The problem is the next plane is on Saturday, the one I have a seat on. I am barely through half the week.

I try to sleep, but do not get much that night. I know I have to do something else to protect myself. After all, my brothers and father taught me how to protect myself. Some of the things I know have to work. That morning I meet a man from New Jersey. His name is Brad, and he is very friendly in a safe way. I tell him about Juan, and Brad says he will keep an eye out for him.

I fill in Cheryl too. And I decide it will be better for me to hang out with Brad for the rest of the week, and I tell Cheryl she is welcome to join us. She did at first, and then it is mainly Brad and

I that spend time together. I am having trouble eating and sleeping. I am a nervous wreck, especially when I am alone.

Brad offers to speak with the Club Fun manager and finds out this is not the first time they have had trouble with Juan stalking the guests. The manager tells Brad that Juan is harmless and will never hurt anyone. And that stalking is a serious accusation and Juan is just trying to be friendly.

Brad thinks this is appalling that the rules in Club Fun are too loose and that they do not care about making their guests feel safe and comfortable. I tell him I have begun leaving hangers on the floor near the entrance of my room. I think it will be a good indicator if while I am gone someone has come into the room, or is still there. That evening Brad walks me to my room. When I open the door, it is instantly obvious that someone has been there.

Brad does not want to leave me alone. I am grateful for that. The room is small. The door opens to the right and beyond that there are two twin beds, one against each wall, with a small dresser between them and a window above the dresser. To the left of the main door is a bathroom.

There are three nights left until I can go home. Brad stays with me the next three nights and makes sure that we get to the transportation that takes us to the plane on Saturday without any problems. I still am not sleeping or eating well, and I am ecstatic to be going home.

38

I call George Newman, my real estate agent and friend while I am at Club Fun and ask him to pick me up at the airport. By this point my parents are living in Florida full-time, but I do not want them to see me in the condition that I am in—no sleep, thin and drawn. George meets me at the gate and drives me to my condo.

Even though I am glad to be home and so appreciate that George picked me up, I do not want to be alone; but I feel like George has done enough for me. He brings my luggage in and stays as I am settling in. He gives me a big hug and says to call him if I need anything else. He is such a good friend.

I have trouble sleeping that night; every little noise scares me. I check to be sure the front door has the bolt on it and that the glass slider is also secure. I keep thinking about my trip to Turks and Caicos and that Juan is probably going to stalk some other woman that arrives at the island today.

In the morning, I wake up feeling thankful to be home. I shower and decide to go out and do some errands. I need to go to the mall and buy a gift for my niece Jill; she is going to be ten. I go shopping at a huge indoor mall that is close to home.

After finding a parking spot, which is always difficult on a Saturday, I walk into the mall. I want to buy Jill some clothes for her birthday. As I am walking through the mall, I see a man that reminds me of Juan. He is my height, medium build with dread locks in his hair too. I get this sick feeling in the pit of my stomach and stand there and freeze. He walks right by me and I start to breathe again.

I have to get out of the mall immediately. What if there are other men who look like him? Are they everywhere? I go back to my car and drive straight home. Realizing that being out in public right now is not a good idea, I decide to call Carl. Earlier in the month I saw Carl before leaving for my Club Fun vacation, I mean nightmare.

Carl is good about calling me back. He asks what is wrong and I give him a brief description of my trip and how I react to seeing the guy with dreadlocks at the mall. And that I feel like I need to stay home for a while. Carl suggests that I call some of my friends and ask them to keep me company and to stay with me all night if possible.

I take Carl's advice and start calling friends. Most of my friends are men. This has always been the way it is. I feel safer with men, especially the way I am feeling right now. I call George, Joe and Ken. You know George. Joe is a close friend of mine that I go dancing with and Ken owns a jewelry store. I shop and have jewelry repaired at his store, and we become friends.

George already knows the situation; I call him first. He suggests that I have the three of them rotate for the next six nights, until I begin feeling safe again. I think this is a great idea. I call Joe and Ken. They are sorry to hear about my trip and will be happy to help.

I call Sam as well. He is angry at me for going to Turks and Caicos in the first place and doesn't want to hear about it. He says I did not listen to his warnings and that he does not want to deal with me or my situation. That is the end of that.

*

I go see Carl the following Monday at his office. He says he did not realize on the phone how badly the trip had affected me. When we spoke on Saturday, he said it sounded like a made-for-TV movie. But then when he sees me in person, he has a better picture of what really went on.

I don't look very well. I have lost weight, down to one hundred and ten pounds, losing seven pounds in one week. I have not put any weight back on yet. Carl has concerns and wants me to see him again later that week. He tells me I should concentrate on gaining some weight and spend time planning my meals in advance and eating, even if I am not hungry.

When I return to Carl's office later that week, I have put two pounds back on. He is happy with the progress. He tells me that my reaction to seeing the man at the mall who reminds me of Juan from the island is not unusual given the circumstances. And that it will take time to heal and feel safe again.

I know he is right, but also know that I will not be taking any trips alone again, that is not any *vacations* alone again. George, Joe and Ken are true friends. The six nights pass. They stop staying over, but remain in close contact. I am fortunate to have such a strong network.

My friend Maggie suggests I get a pet. She thinks it will be good for me and comfort me when I am alone. This is great advice. I know of a woman who takes in stray cats. I call her and ask her if she has a kitten that I can adopt. She says she has a black and white kitten. I ask her what the cost is, and she asks me to bring cat supplies for her other cats instead of paying her.

I have no experience with pets. We never had any growing up and I was an infant when my mom flushed the fish down the toilet. I go to the pet store and buy food for the cat lady and a pet taxi to bring my new kitten home, along with all the other supplies I need—a litter box, litter, bowls for food and water, etc.

When I arrive at the cat lady's house, it is something I have never seen before. She has litter boxes up and down the hallway; there must be a dozen all together. She tells me that she has twenty cats and the one kitten I am going to adopt. She takes me into a bedroom. There is chair, similar to a dining room chair, and the kitten is hiding under it. The cat lady picks her up and hands her to me.

The kitten is adorable, a tuxedo cat, black fur with white paws and a white ribbon of fur around the kitten's neck and some white markings on the face. The cat lady does not know if the kitten is female or male. My new veterinarian will have to tell me.

Off we go, me and my new friend, to the vet's office. He examines the kitten and says she is a female and is probably 8 to

10 weeks old. The cat lady says she found the kitten at a mall parking lot all alone.

I decide to name my kitten Precious. My brother Warren also has a cat named Precious, and I love the name and think it is perfect for her. The first few nights are a little rocky. Precious likes to stay up all night and meow and walk on the bed and wake me up and keep me up most of the night. I call the vet and he suggests that I lock her up in a room at night so she can learn that it is the time she needs to sleep, so that she will be awake during the day. This is difficult to do; I really do not want to lock her up in my bathroom. But at least her litter box is in there too.

After locking Precious in the bathroom for three nights, she is trained! Thank goodness, because I am not sure I am cut out to be a pet owner. I really need my sleep. Now that she settles into a better routine, we become very close. She is such good company. She gives me unconditional love, and I love her back the same way; she is a comfort to me.

39

After a couple of months, I decide I want to start dating again. After my experience with Sam Camel, I think it is best to throw out the letters from the personal ad. I am going back to the original dating service; I believe they can help me.

I call the dating service and they tell me about a man who has just become a member with the service, and they feel we are a good match.

At the time, I am still working for my client Dr. Ned Yearly, who is a pulmonary specialist. His billing staff never resubmitted claims that had been rejected. His claims are large, because he has many hospital patients. He hires me to clear up this problem. His receivables are over $100,000 behind.

I have been doing work for Ned for over a year, and I am ready to look for a new client. I receive a referral to Richard Brown, MD, from a client of mine. Richard is starting from scratch. He just completed his residency in Internal Medicine. He hires me to set up his practice, decorate the waiting room, hire the employees and train them.

The dating service asks for permission to give my phone number to Ron, Ron Thomas. He calls me that evening. It sounds like we have a lot in common. I tell him that I work close to the high-rise apartment building where he lives. We decide to meet at an Italian restaurant.

Ron is an appellate attorney and is very conservative. He drives a late model four-door Chrysler, the kind your grandmother drives. He is almost six feet tall, medium build, salt and pepper hair and wears silver metal glasses. He is three years older than me.

Dinner is delicious. I have eaten at this Italian restaurant before; they have the best gorgonzola salad and luscious hot garlic rolls dripping in butter, a real treat.

Ron tells me about his family. He has one younger sister, Joyce, and a brother-in-law. They have a young son, and they live near my condo. Ron tells me that his mother passed away several years before. She died from breast cancer.

Ron's father has since remarried. They are a very tight-knit family and see each other at least once a week. I have concerns about this after experiencing the smothering I received from my family and Jack's as well.

Ron and I enjoy a lot of the same things. Good food, travel, walking on the beach, spending time outdoors and going to the movies. We start seeing each other exclusively fairly soon after we meet. We are looking for the same things, a stable relationship, marriage and children. Ron loves to go out to eat all the time. As a matter of fact, he cannot cook at all. And he feels we both work hard, so going out to eat is the thing to do.

I meet Ron's family early in our relationship. His father is a wonderful man, full of life and clearly a good person. Sarah is his stepmother, and is very sweet. And I am happy to meet his sister Joyce, always welcoming someone new in my life. We all got along wonderfully and Ron is happy about that.

Things move along nicely. For my thirtieth birthday, Ron surprises me with a dozen roses and a limo ride to a gourmet restaurant. He presents me with a marcasite bracelet. It is made with links that are hearts. It is beautiful and I ask Ron to put it on my wrist.

I am very comfortable in our relationship. I spend the night at Ron's apartment during the week, while I am working for my client. Ron spends the weekend at my condo and we often get together with his sister and her husband.

Ron soon gives me a key to his apartment. That is only because I leave for work later than him and he wants me to be able to lock the dead bolt, even though there is another lock on the knob that secures his apartment door. He is a bit controlling. Ron calls me at work and asks me if I have not only bolted the door to his apartment, but have put away the blow dryer after using it.

After we had been dating for two years, Ron tells me he very much wants to marry me and get engaged in the next several months. I feel the same way. We have been living together most of the time, and we are in love and compatible. Then things begin to unravel. I am having some difficultly with my bladder. I still saw Dr. Smyth twice a year. I was due for my yearly GYN exam and tell my gynecologist that I think I have a bladder infection. He asks me to leave a urine specimen. He tells me that the specimen is clear, but the nurse will send it out for a culture.

A urine culture is a test to find and identify germs that may be causing a urinary tract infection. A urine sample is kept under conditions that allow bacteria to grow for 24 hours. If few bacteria grow, the test is negative; if many grow the test is positive and will require prescribing an antibiotic.

I wait for a call from Dr. Gordon, my gynecologist, about the urine culture results. I am unsure that this is the right decision though. Dr. Gordon is not my urologist, and having had total bladder failure and being prone to bladder problems, I decide to give my urologist, Dr. Smyth, a call.

Dr. Smyth asks me to meet him at his office that afternoon. I provide him with a fresh urine specimen and wait for him to tell me the results. I press gently on my bladder to help empty it, as Dr. Smyth has taught me to do. He says after looking at the specimen under the microscope, that he does not like the way it looks, and asks me about all my symptoms again. I tell him I am having an urgency to urinate, but do not feel like I am emptying my bladder. And my stomach hurts on the left side where my bladder is.

He wants to catheterize me in the office. As unpleasant as that is, I know he has to check to see how much residual urine I have. Dr. Smyth is unhappy. He says I have not been emptying my bladder well and am holding too much urine. And before things get worse, he is going to admit me to the hospital. He thinks I may have sepsis. He explains that occasionally urinary tract infections spread into the bloodstream, which can cause serious problems, even death, if treatment isn't aggressive.

I drive myself to the hospital and go straight to the admissions office. Dr. Smyth has called the hospital in advance so the admission process can go quickly, avoiding the emergency room. They take me up to my room and the nurse comes in to start an IV.

Dr. Smyth tells me at his office that the best way to treat sepsis is intravenous antibiotics for at least five days and up to seven days. I have to be in the hospital all that time. I am very unhappy about this and feel like I can't get a break.

I call Ron at home. It is past dinnertime. I tell him that I am going to have to be in the hospital for almost a week. He sounds understanding and says he will be by tomorrow after work to see me. This is probably a bad sign. I sure would be there right away for him if he was in the hospital. After I get off the phone with him, a call comes in. It is Joyce checking to see if I need anything; it is nice to have her support.

It is an uneventful hospital stay, hospital food, reading magazines and books, watching TV and lots of sleep. Visitors come and go—Ron, Joyce, my mother and father. Dr. Smyth comes in every day to check on me. Finally, on the sixth morning he says I can go home. So happy to hear that!

*

Time moves on and Ron and I are going through the motions of our relationship. But that is all it is. He no longer talks about getting engaged, and on weekends he does not include me in all his family gatherings like he has in the past. I approach him about not including me and he makes excuses that there isn't enough room for one more person. Highly unlikely; I see the writing on the wall.

I am still working at Richard Brown's office and have made friends with the dietician we hired for the practice. Her name is Laura Snow. I learn many things from her about nutrition and diet. I tell Laura that I have many healthy recipes, actually a whole bag of them. We decide to write a nutritional cookbook together.

When I am about to leave work an afternoon in September 1988, I get a call from Ron. He asks me to meet him in the parking structure under my client's building. I think this is odd, but I know what is coming. He has been distant, and we aren't connecting. I leave the office and walk down to the parking structure. Ron is there, in his new Volvo. He finally gets rid of his Chrysler and it looks like I am next.

He walks over to me and kisses me on the cheek. That is strange. Then he steps back and says he has something to tell me. He does not think our relationship is working out and that it is over. Since I know this is coming, it is far from shocking, but I feel like I still need to put up a fight. I tell him that I think it is cowardly to break up in a parking lot. He says he doesn't care and goes to his car and hands me a bag of my clothes and personal items that I left at his apartment, and he demands his key.

Ron is a "mama's boy" just like Jack. I know this from the beginning of our relationship and can clearly see that I made the same mistake again. It is hard to admit. This is not going to happen again. I need to finally learn how to stay away from these type of men.

I drive straight home. I decide to have a rest from men for a while. I call a couple of my girlfriends and tell them that Ron has ended our relationship. My friend Maggie says she is happy about the breakup. She feels like Ron kept me away from my friends. There is truth to that. Besides being a mama's boy, he is possessive and controlling.

Maggie offers to fix me up with friends of her boyfriend. I tell her I am taking a break from men, but sure, if she wants to set it up for a couple months from now, that will be fine.

40

The next few months fly by. My friend Joe is glad to hear that Ron and I are over. He asks me out and says he wants to be more than friends. I am not ready to date anyone exclusively. Joe is a great friend and I suggest that we take things slowly and that we can continue dating others.

While at a charity event that my girlfriend Debbie invites me to, I meet an attorney. Oh no, not another one. It seems that they are all professional liars. Mike is very charismatic and fun. He asks me out and I accept. We meet for dinner. He is a smooth talker and suggests that on our next date he wants to show me his cooking skills. I am not going to fall for that.

Mike tells me that his next-door neighbor is Phillip Michael Thomas from the TV show *Miami Vice*. Somehow that does not impress me, and I suggest that we can meet for dinner again soon.

I am still working in North Miami at Richard Brown's office. There is a private singles party two minutes from my condo on the last Wednesday of March in 1989. I mention it to my mother and she encourages me to go. Sometimes her advice is good; this is one of these times.

I drive home from my client's office and stop at my condo to change. I put on a black miniskirt, a black and white top with a checkered design, and three-inch black pumps. The party is at a restaurant and bar. I walk in and order a drink, vodka and cranberry on the rocks, with a twist of lime. I look around the room and recognize most of the people there.

Then I notice two guys who I have not seen before sitting at a table for three. It is one of those high tables you see at bars. I do the once around the room to say hi to friends and people I know and then walk over to the table with the two guys. I ask if the open seat is available. Both of them smile and say yes, please join them.

Their names are Jim and David. They are both friendly and Jim explains that David is new in town. That he is a consultant from the DC area who is working with him. It is a three-year commitment and David flies back to DC every weekend.

We all begin sharing stories of who we might know in common. Time is flying and I am glad I have come to this party. David excuses himself for a moment and while he is away from the table Jim asks me for my phone number. I do not give it to him.

When David returns, he asks me about my family and where I am from. David never stops smiling the whole time. He is dark and handsome, with brown eyes that smile at me, and dark brown hair, almost black. He is wearing casual clothes, a polo shirt, khakis and cordovan loafers. I ask him how old he is, and he says 31. I am happy to hear this, as he looks younger. I tell him I think he is in his mid-twenties. I share with him that I am 31 as well.

I tell David about being from the Midwest and that I have lived in Florida for seven years, but that I miss the north and the change of seasons. What I do not share right away is how much I miss northern men, and that the men in Florida are different, plastic and not down to earth. We share information about our careers. I also tell him that I have a cat, Precious, who I adopted. This seems important to David.

It has been two hours since we all started talking and the party is breaking up. We all stand up to leave. I am looking at David and realize I am taller than him, being that this is the first time we are standing up next to each other, I say, "Oh, I'm wearing three-inch heels." He laughs and says he wants tall offspring. Wow that is a lot of information for just meeting someone new. I smile and we all walk out of the restaurant.

David and Jim both offer to walk me to my car. On the way David asks me for my phone number. This is a relief, because I am not really into Jim. David is so full of life, and that smile. He is so handsome. David says he is going back to DC for the weekend and will call me from there. Sounds good.

David is true to his word and calls me Saturday morning and asks me out for dinner on Monday night. I am happy and call my mother to tell her. She thinks it all sounds great, but still prefers someone at least six feet tall for me. You can tell what her priorities are.

David calls again on Sunday, telling me he is so sorry, but can we change our dinner date to Tuesday. His favorite basketball team is in the playoffs on Monday night and he and his buddies want to watch the game. David invites me to join them. I thank him and decline the invitation; it doesn't feel safe going to his apartment with a bunch of guys I don't know.

I did feel comfortable enough to have David pick me up at my condo. He arrives at 6:30 p.m. on Tuesday. I show him around my tiny place, which takes all of two minutes and we end up in the kitchen. I keep looking at his face, his skin; it looks like he has no facial hair. His skin is smooth as silk and looks so soft I want to touch his face. I hold off on that and we leave for dinner.

We have a delicious dinner. David has a ravenous appetite, and before I know it, he is done with his dinner. Kiddingly I tell him that just watching him eat; one can get indigestion. He laughs and tells me that as a kid he went to overnight camp for the whole summer. And that he was a waiter there. David explained that in order to be sure there was food for the waiters to eat; they had to serve the campers, counselors, etc., quickly and run back to the kitchen for their meals. It stuck and this is the way he continues to eat.

After dinner we walk around. David holds my hand, and it feels very right. He tells me he plans to stay in Florida for the weekend and not return to DC. He invites me to have brunch with him on Sunday. I accept. He drives me back home and gives me a gentle kiss on the lips and off he goes.

I am still seeing Joe and Mike, but my interest is in David. I have a date with Mike on Friday night. It is already Wednesday and I have not heard from Mike yet. David calls me at my new client. He says he knows it is late in the week, am I available on

Friday for a date? I tell him I will have to get back with him, as I have other plans, but they are not confirmed yet.

I immediately call Mike. He answers and I tell him I have to cancel our plans for Friday. He asks why and I tell him directly that I am dating someone else and am moving on. He asks me if I am sure and I tell him absolutely. I then call David back and tell him I am now free on Friday. He is happy and asks me what I want to do,

"I hear that there is a Spinners concert on Friday; how does that sound?"

He says sure. He picks me up at my condo and again I notice that his face is totally smooth. I ask him if he has facial hair. He laughs and says he lots of it and that it is very dark, but that he shaves twice a day when we have dates. What an honor.

David has a different rental car each week. This week he has a Chrysler LeBaron white convertible with red leather interior. It is a forty-five-minute ride to the concert. We drive with the top down and as we drive, the sun is setting. It is a gorgeous spring night in Florida. I am wearing white slacks with a mint green and white cotton sweater. David is wearing khakis and a polo shirt, which seems to be his uniform. I like it.

The concert is wonderful. It has been a while since I have seen a Motown group perform. They sing, "Mighty Love," "One of a Kind Love Affair," "Sadie" and "Rubberband Man," to name a few of my favorites. David really enjoys the concert as well. It is a magical evening.

Afterwards we go out for dinner at a local diner. We have to wait in line at least thirty minutes to get a table. There are three lines; one for the counter, one for two people at a table and one for four or more people.

That Friday evening when David and I arrive, there is only one person waiting in the counter line and we decide that is the best choice for us. We are soon seated at the counter. I tell him about the great sandwiches and the mile-high lemon meringue pie. He suggests we get an order of each and split them. That sounds perfect to me.

Our sandwich comes and it is so thick I have difficultly opening my mouth wide enough to take a bite. David did not have this problem! We thoroughly enjoy it. Next the mile-high lemon meringue pie. I do not have a ruler with me, but it easily measures four to five inches high and it is amazing and delicious!

We drive home from the beaches, David keeping his eyes on the road and I watch the sky and try to count the stars. It is a perfect evening. I don't want it to end. David walks me to my door and again gives me a soft kiss on the lips and says he will pick me up at eleven on Sunday for brunch. He is the perfect gentleman.

*

I often have lunch with my parents on Saturday and cannot stop talking about David. My mother asks me what about Mike and Joe? I tell her that I am only seeing David and that Joe will always be my friend. My parents want the same thing for me that I want, a good marriage, a family and to be happy and healthy. At least that is how it feels right now.

One thing is for sure, my parents have a good marriage. They are very much in tune with each other and never fight. Perhaps part of the reason for this is my mother is controlling and manipulating and my dad gives in to her. The only memories I have as a child of them arguing is when something very challenging was happening to our family. Warren was in a bad car accident. He was driving home from college with a couple of buddies and they kept switching drivers, and eventually the driver fell asleep at the wheel and Warren's car hit an embankment and rolled over and landed on the hood. No one was badly injured, but Warren being so tall, six foot, four, did have some chronic back pain.

David comes by to pick me up at eleven on Sunday morning. We go to a local pancake house for breakfast. We spend the rest of the day at an art show in the town next to mine. There are barriers to close the road to local traffic, allowing the artists to set up their displays in the middle of the street.

We walk around for a long time looking closely at all the paintings and jewelry. I buy a pair of silver earrings from one of the artists. All of the artists have tents set up over their wares and that is a good thing. Out of nowhere a thunderstorm begins and the rain comes down in buckets. David and I run for shelter. I am not feeling well after that, dizzy, as if I might faint, and David says, "Wow, it is five o'clock and we have not eaten anything since brunch. Let's get you something to eat and you will feel better." He is right and from then on David insists I carry a snack bag in the car for this exact purpose. I appreciate the way he takes care of me.

We see each other again for dinner on Tuesday of the following week. David asks me if I want to come home with him to DC for the weekend. I have never been to Washington, DC and am certainly up for it. I mention to him we have only been dating a couple of weeks and is he sure about the invitation? He is sure. So that Friday I bring a small suitcase to my client's office. I am going to meet David at his apartment which, is closer to the airport and then we will drive there together.

We land at National Airport in DC. David's car is in the parking lot at the airport. He drives me around DC. It is mid-April and some of the cherry blossoms are still on the trees. We drive by the Jefferson Memorial and the Mall, where the Smithsonian is, along with many museums that we will visit over the weekend.

David had moved out of his apartment when he knew that he would be in Florida for three years at the client site. He put all his things in storage and rented a room from a guy that he works with in DC. It is in a townhouse in Virginia. We drive there for the night. We had been intimate right before leaving for DC. I feel comfortable staying with David at his buddy's apartment.

First thing in the morning we are off on my adventure. David assures me that he will take me on a fabulous tour of DC and explains that two days are hardly enough time to see everything. He says that it will take a month, but promises to bring me back again to see more in the future. The first place David takes me is to a small museum, the hologram museum. It is very interesting, and then we move on to Air and Space at the Smithsonian, David's favorite museum. It is outstanding. We see the Apollo 11 space capsule, the Wright brothers' plane, a Goddard rocket, the Spirit of St. Louis airplane and much more.

Next we go to the National Gallery of Art, which quickly becomes my favorite. There are so many exhibits to see: "Cezanne: The Early Years," Rembrandt and many other famous artists. From there we go to the Capitol. Of course, this is another first for me. When we walk into the rotunda, I start to cry. It is overwhelming the feeling of power that comes from the room. The pride wells up in me knowing how lucky I am to be an American.

David holds my hand and leads me through the rest of the Capitol for an expert tour. We see the Statue of Freedom and where the Senate and the Congress meet, the Constitution and more. We then walk up the whole Mall to the Washington Monument. What an unbelievable site.

David wants to take me to the Whitney Museum, one of his favorites. He shares with me for the first time that he had a cat named Whitney, after the museum. Unfortunately, she had gotten out of his apartment and after a long search he did not find her and she did not return home on her own. Now I knew why he was so pleased that I adopted my cat.

We go to Adams Morgan for dinner. Adams Morgan is a neighborhood in NW DC. It has major night life with many bars and restaurants, David asks me if it is OK to invite his friend James to have dinner with us. I think it will be great to meet a friend of David's. It turns out that James actually is a professor of David's from college. James is a Harvard graduate and is a wealth of knowledge.

After dinner James says good night and David wants to take me to the Roxy for reggae night. He tells me that every Saturday is reggae night and that is his favorite kind of music. That is where we go. The Roxy looks like an old movie theater that is now a dance club. There is dancing on the first floor and the reggae band is playing on the second floor.

I am happy to be learning more and more about David. He is a great reggae dancer and teaches me how to do it. We stand side by side and he plants his feet on the ground and just lets his body sway to the music. It isn't hard to do, but fun. I love seeing all these different sides of David.

The next day we continue on my tour of DC. We go to the Lincoln Memorial, visit the Arlington Cemetery and walk by the White House in the morning. In the afternoon David takes me to the National Zoo. We both love animals and I can't wait to see the giraffes. Giraffe was a nickname I was given in sixth grade, because I was five feet, six when I was twelve, which was a head taller than all of my friends who later all caught up to me. I never minded the nickname, and when it wore off, giraffes became my favorite animal.

We take the metro system during our tour and it is fascinating as well. When you walk into the metro station, there is an escalator that goes down into the earth, two to three flights down, straight down. It is scary at first. We arrive at the stop for the zoo. It is a hot day in April. I want to see the giraffes first, so off we go in the direction the signs point us to. When we get there, no giraffes; there is a sign saying that a renovation is taking place and the giraffes are staying at another zoo for the time being. This is a disappointment for both of us. David so wants to please me.

We take a late flight back to Florida. It has been an amazing weekend. David is so much fun to be with and there is never a dull moment. He has endless energy; I don't know anyone like him. Usually it is my friends who have trouble keeping up with me. It looks like I have met my match.

41

On the Tuesday evening after we get back, we have dinner again. During dinner, David suggests that he bring his computer to my condo, so we will have more time together, even if some of the time he has to do work. And he asks me if I mind if he brings his laundry to do as well. I think about this and am taken aback a bit. It seems like things are moving very quickly. He points out that after all, we are both 31 and know what we want from life. David tells me if he met me a couple of years ago, he wouldn't have been ready to settle down. He knows now is the right time.

I feel safe with David, which is very important to me after all I have been through in relationships. He is kind, funny, a great listener. He is also becoming my best friend, along with being my boyfriend. I know this is the right way to start a new relationship.

The next day David brings his computer over to my condo. He sets it up on an extra table I have in the living room by the glass sliding door. He puts the computer monitor on the table and the computer tower on the floor. After this is all set up, he goes back to his car to get his laundry. I show him where I keep all the laundry supplies, so he can feel at home.

*

In early May David asks if he can move in with me. He sees no point in going to his apartment and spending time with his work buddies. It feels like a fine idea. A couple of days later, we are living together.

One day very soon after David moves in completely, he comes home from his client and announces that he is going to Rio de Janeiro in two weeks. He tells me that two of the consultants he is working with, Hector and Carlos, are from Rio. They are returning home for a visit and want David to join them.

David asks me if I want to go with him to Rio. I stand there and am not sure what to say. David and I have known each other less than six weeks. He has already taken me to DC for a whirlwind tour, we are living together, and now he is asking if I want to go with him to Rio, as if he is asking me out for ice cream. I finally respond and say, "Really?" and he says "Sure." This is something new for me.

With David it is second nature for him to include me in his plans and mean it. I call my client and ask for the time off. Since they are paying me by the hour, they have no problem with it. Great! Next David says he wants to pay for half my airplane ticket, since it is such short notice. This is generous. I accept after he keeps insisting.

Next David tells me that Hector has a cousin, Marco, who owns a condo that is empty. He offers it to David and me for our visit to Rio. That is also very generous. The next two weeks are all about getting ready for our trip. Hector and Carlos have told us to leave all jewelry and expensive cameras at home. And that David has to buy a Speedo bathing suit, because that is the only kind that Brazilian men wear.

The flight to Rio is direct from Florida. We both have current passports and off we go. When we arrive in Rio, Hector picks us up at the airport and takes us back to his parents' home. They are lovely people and offer us a delicious meal. During dinner, not only do we meet Hector's parents, we meet Marco, Carlos' cousin. Marco says he has bad news for us, that two weeks lead time is not enough time for the electric company to turn on the electricity in his condo and it will be at least another two weeks.

Hector has a solution. He says that David can stay at his parents' home and I can stay at Marco's apartment. Not wanting to cause any trouble, David says that might work. I excuse myself and take David with me to the hallway to talk about it. We both know it isn't a great plan and we need to come up with a better solution. We ask Hector what a hotel costs. He tells us that any well-known hotel, such as the Sheraton, is costly.

Hector suggests a small hotel three blocks from Ipanema Beach that Brazilian businessmen frequent. He phones there for us to find out if they have availability and what the cost is. They did have a room available and the cost is twenty American dollars a night. Fantastic, we hit the jackpot. I tell David that I insist on paying for the room. David finally agrees and off we go with our luggage to the hotel.

Hector helps us check in, since neither David nor I speak Portuguese. We thank Hector for all his help and walk over to the elevator. It is a small old-fashioned elevator with an accordion-like doorway that you push to one side and then enter the elevator. We are on the third of four floors.

We enter our room and there is a small amount of furniture. There is a bed, a very hard bed. The mattress has no give whatsoever. I hear this is common in Brazil, keeping in mind if this was a more American-style hotel the mattress may be softer. There is a small window and a dresser with a mirror over it, no TV, and one lamp that is screwed to the wall over the bed. There is also a refrigerator with bottled water in it, as it isn't safe to drink the tap water. A small bathroom includes a sink, no countertop and a small mirror over it, with a stall shower that is tiny, just right for us to take a shower together.

Believe me we aren't complaining about the accommodations. It is a wonderful alternative to staying at separate homes for the week. We wake early and go downstairs for breakfast. The bar doubles as a breakfast area in the morning. Again, there is a language barrier, so we point to foods. We have freshly made yogurt with nuts and berries. We have *mamão*, Portuguese for papaya, and crusty rolls with sweet butter and a tall glass of milk. Neither David nor I drink coffee.

David goes to pay the check and we find out that breakfast is part of the daily room charge, and that it is customary to tip the waitress at the end of our trip. That is exactly what David does. At the end of our stay he gives the waitress a twenty-dollar bill. The expression on her face is priceless; she is smiling ear to ear. She has her boss translate to us that is what she makes each week being a waitress, twenty dollars.

*

169

We spend the whole day at Ipanema Beach. We walk there from the hotel and lay in the sun and swim. It is a wonderful day. Yes, it is true all the guys on the beach are wearing Speedo bathing suits. David fits right in. And for more than one reason; he has that olive complexion, and no one thinks he is American. Now I am a different story. Blonde hair and blue eyes...I do not fit right in.

On our walk back to the hotel, we stop at the street markets and sample fresh fruits and vegetables. We find exotic fruits that we have never seen before, with names we cannot pronounce. We buy oranges, grapes, apples, tiny bananas and strawberries to take back to our hotel room.

The next morning we take a ride up to Sugarloaf Mountain. Rio is built in a valley with two mountains on either side of it; one of them is Sugar Loaf. Reaching the top of Sugar Loaf is a two-step process. You take a cable car for over seven hundred feet with a view of Corcovado Mountain and Guanabara Bay. Then we transfer to a second cable car that takes us thirteen hundred feet to the top, where there are magnificent views of Copacabana. The whole experience is breathtaking.

That evening we have dinner with both Hector and Carlos. They take us to a churrasco, known to us Americans as a Brazilian bar-be-que. The meat is cooked over coals, on a skewer. The seasoning is coarse salt. The meats include pork tenderloin, all different cuts of beef, chicken and sausages. The waiter brings the meat to the table on the skewer and asks you how much you want. Then places the sharp end of the skewer on the plate and takes a knife and pushes the pieces of meat onto your plate.

Hector orders drinks for the table. He picks cachaça, liquor made out of sugarcane. It is similar to rum. I don't like hard liquor, but I do try it. It tastes like pure alcohol and smells just like rubbing alcohol. The guys all drink it, including David, who never wants to offend his friends by not joining in.

We all take a cab back to our hotel after dinner. Hector, David and I are sitting in the backseat of the cab and Carlos is in the front. When the cab driver pulls up in front of the hotel, Hector gets out first, then I do and then David. In a split-second someone runs up to me and tries pulling my purse off my arm, even though I have men surrounding me. Both David and Hector come to my rescue and the purse snatcher runs off without my purse.

David and I know that Rio can be dangerous, especially at night. We think we are safe going out in a group. Right above the hotel in the distance are the *favelas*, which means slums in Portuguese. People live in small houses in close proximity. The *favelas* have a wall with cement to glue the broken glass onto the ledge of the wall, making it unsafe to try to climb in or out. I feel so badly for these people. They live in poverty and most likely feel desperate at times.

The next day after having our special breakfast, we are off for a tour to the countryside. I quickly realize the poverty that exists in and outside of Rio. As the bus drives by farms, we stop at one and visit the farmstand there. I immediately notice the small children begging the tourists for money and the babies running around without any clothing on. It is sad and helps me appreciate what I have.

After the tour we go to an Italian restaurant for dinner. The food is outstanding. First we have antipasto. The food is beautifully displayed on a large platter. There are bell peppers, mushrooms, pepperoncini, olives, artichoke hearts, provolone and mozzarella cheese. Everything is so fresh. I am beginning to believe that Rio has some of the best food I have ever tasted.

The next morning, we take a train to Christ Mountain. That is what Hector calls it. The full name of the statue is Christ the Redeemer on top of the mountain. The statue of Christ is over one hundred feet tall, with outstretched arms. It stands on top of Corcovado Mountain and has hundreds of visitors a year, tourists and locals. You can see the entire city from there on a clear day— the beaches, mountains and the *favelas*. It is another outstanding experience.

It is time to pack and fly back to Florida. We spend the last night in Rio taking Hector, Carlos and Marco out for dinner. We go to a disco after dinner, and the DJ is playing Rick Astley. I love his voice and singing style and my favorites are "Never Gonna Give You Up," "Together Forever" and "You Move Me."

The plane ride back to Florida is quiet. We get blankets and pillows as we board the plane. David and I snuggle together the whole way home. It has been an amazing and glorious trip. Like a dream. David is opening new doors for me, teaching me and showing me so many exciting places in the world. What a gift.

42

In the weeks following I visit two more cities with David that are both new to me. He takes me to Philadelphia for a reunion at his prep school, one of the oldest prep schools in the area. Just as one imagines; two- and three-story stone-front buildings with ivy climbing up the walls. The wood steps of the stairway in the main building of the school are worn down, as if the wood has been carefully scooped out.

David attended this school from fourth through twelfth grade. He was so fortunate to be able to attend a school that prepared him so well for his college career and beyond. It was an all-boys prep school; his graduating class had seventy-nine students. I was impressed with the way David focused on whatever goal he was achieving. He gave more than 110% to it, and I so respected that about him.

We also go to Durham, North Carolina, for his MBA college reunion. Duke's campus is so beautiful. The garden beds are full of flowers, in vibrant colors, along with lush landscaping everywhere. David takes me inside the chapel to see it. He tells me in advance that weddings often take place there on weekends. This is one of those weekends. We quietly walk in. People are scurrying around preparing the chapel for a wedding, running wide white ribbons from pew to pew, placing flowers on pedestals. It is a sight to see.

One weekend David suggests we take at a small cruise ship to the Bahamas. Let me reiterate it is a *small* cruise ship. I call it a boat not a ship. As it is on many Florida summer days, rain is in the forecast. David and I drive to the port and are going to sail to the Bahamas for the weekend. Things go smoothly at first, then the clouds get dark and the thunder begins. The boat starts to sway. We are down below in a cabin and I start to feel nauseous. David insists we go up to the deck and sit there, so that I can watch the horizon and that I will feel less nauseous.

David loves to sail and he has all these tricks up his sleeve. He is right, and up on deck, I begin to feel better. I have my head in David's lap and am watching the horizon. David is my hero! More than half of the people are seasick that day on the way to the Bahamas. When we arrive at the hotel and casino, we go to the room for a short nap. Later we gamble a bit and enjoy a light dinner together. The next day we spend time on the beach, and in the early evening cruise back to Florida.

Fortunately, the waters are calm and it is smooth sailing getting home. David suggests that we take cruises off of our list of future vacations. I remind him it is really not a cruise ship. But we both agree that there is too much food available on a cruise, the perfect formula for coming home ten pounds heavier. We both are health conscious and decide to find destinations on dry land.

Soon after, David's client Sam invites us to his home on Marathon Key. The Florida Keys are so special. I have been there many times before, but it is a whole new experience with David. We drive down to Marathon in one of his rental convertibles and have a wonderful time. We watch the sunset after a fabulous bar-be-que dinner. Sam grills fresh snapper that he has caught earlier in the day. It melts in your mouth. Salad and margaritas accompany the snapper. Watermelon is for dessert. It is a relaxing and rejuvenating day, very special getting away to the Keys.

The next morning, we drive down to Key West for the day and have lunch at Sloppy Joes. In December of 1933, prohibition was repealed and that is when Sloppy Joes opened. Ernest Hemingway often spent time there. It is a historic spot. After lunch we visit Ernest Hemingway's home, which is now a museum. For me the most interesting part of the tour is hearing how Hemingway loved cats. And dozens of them lived on the property.

Hemingway had been given a six toed cat as a present. Most cats have five toes in the front and four toes in the back, so it was unusual for a cat to have six toes. Many of Hemingway's cats inherited this trait. Even today any cat that has six toes is said to be related to his cats.

*

Before meeting David, I made plans to visit my oldest brother Lee, my sister-in-law Lois and their daughters in Disney World. I do not want to drive the four hours each way, so I make an airline reservation. It is an exciting time knowing I will be spending it with my nieces Jill and Jennifer.

I ask David to join me, but there are no seats left on the plane. He suggests that I fly to Orlando and that he drives there and meets me. Then we can drive back home together. Nothing seems to faze David; he always has a practical solution. I really like that.

Our plan is to meet for breakfast at Disney World in the Magic Kingdom and have Mickey Mouse waffles. The night before, I spent time with Lee, Lois and the girls. I share a room with Jill and Jennifer. It is wonderful to see them and have so much quality time to catch up. We wake up and get ready for the day and take the monorail to the Magic Kingdom.

We are all seated in the restaurant at 8:50 a.m. David plans to arrive at 9:00 am, and sure enough at 9 on the nose, he walks up to our table and gives me a kiss on the cheek. I find it amazing and am in awe that anyone can be so prompt, especially in Disney World. If he is trying to impress me, it is working.

Lee and his family are the first to meet David, besides my parents. We have a fun day in the Magic Kingdom and at Epcot. Living in Florida I have been to Disney World many times, but this time is the most special, sharing it with David and my family.

After lots of discussion we all decide to go to the Grand Floridian for dinner. The Grand Floridian is a copy of the Grand Hotel on Mackinac Island in the upper peninsula of Michigan. Growing up in the Midwest, I was lucky enough to visit Mackinac Island and see the Grand Hotel. The movie *Somewhere in Time*, with Jane Seymour and Christopher Reeve was filmed there.

What is so striking about Mackinac Island is that there is a no-car rule; you take a ferry from the mainland to the island. It certainly is like stepping back in time, taking a ride on a horse-drawn carriage, or riding a bicycle, so very relaxing.

Dinner is interesting. I order a glass of wine and the waiter cards me. I am 31. My sister-in-law Lois, who is seven years older than I am, isn't happy about it. The waiter does not card her. We all enjoy fresh seafood dinners, and it is nice having David meet part of my family.

After dinner, Lois and I are standing talking and she says how wonderful it is that in such a short time, David has taken me to DC and Rio and now meets me here in Disney World. I should hang on to him! Lee offers to have us stay with them at their hotel. David has already made a reservation at the same hotel for us, so we all take the monorail back after an incredible day and say our good-byes.

43

Weeks go by and David and I fall more in love every day. He is so easy to be with and he tells me repeatedly that he loves my company. It amazes me how he follows me around my one-bedroom condo just to be with me. Life is so full with David in my world.

My birthday is around the corner. David asks me if I want to go to New York City to celebrate. I have never been to New York, what a great idea. Of course going up north during late December will mean that it will be cold. I have to find my winter clothes and coats; it has been almost ten years since I saw snow.

We fly to New York and take a cab to the Marriott Marquis in Times Square. It is a bit overwhelming, never having been to New York City before, all the hustle and bustle, especially at Christmas time. The streets are full of people and the store windows have beautiful decorations and sparkling lights.

We check into the hotel and go right up to our room. I pull the curtains back and see we have a view of Times Square. I think it will be breathtaking on New Year's Eve. David suggests we go to a steakhouse. We have fabulous filet mignon and onion rings. The filet melts in my mouth like butter. David is happy to see how much I am enjoying our visit to NYC in just the few hours we have been there.

The next day we to meet Jim, David's associate from work, the same Jim that I met when I met David. Jim is dating a woman he met in Florida who is originally from New York. We have lunch together. It is great fun sharing the afternoon with Jim and Debbie. After lunch we see a Sondheim musical together. My first Broadway show. It all seems so surreal.

That evening we go to David's brother's home outside of the city. This is the first time I am meeting Henry, his wife Cathy and their two children Ken and Sally. They live in an exquisite house and make me feel very welcome. David is especially close with Cathy. He also has taken Ken on several weekend visits to DC.

The next day is my birthday. We get up late and go for brunch. David and I roam around Manhattan, spending part of the day walking through Central Park and visiting the Metropolitan Museum of Art and the American Museum of Natural History. We have a light dinner and return to the hotel.

I am sound asleep and David wakes me at midnight, when my birthday is ending and the next day marks our nine-month anniversary. He asks me to marry him. I say "YES," we kiss, and then go back to sleep.

The next morning David takes me to the diamond district to pick out an engagement ring. We visit several different stores and pick a round diamond with two baguettes on either side of the center stone. The diamond is one karat, and David asks me if that is big enough. I don't know anything else to say except, of course.

We visit the Empire State Building, where David's father has his office. The rest of our trip is a whirlwind, touring different parts of New York and enjoying delicious food. Most of the restaurants are small and cozy, perfect settings for a newly engaged couple.

New Year's Eve is phenomenal. I don't love crowds, or feeling like a sardine. Since David is so thoughtful and arranges a room with a view of Times Square, we are on the fortieth floor and have the perfect seats. We watch the hordes of people from our window and share our first New Year's Eve together, a night to remember.

*

We arrive back in Florida late New Year's Day. David and I have plans to meet my parents for dinner. They do not know about our engagement yet. Both my mom and dad seem genuinely happy for us. My mother wants to know if we have a date for the wedding. We do, the second Sunday in June in 1990, which falls on Father's Day that year. They say they would love to help plan the wedding, as we barely have six months to do it.

My mother and I spend many days searching for the right wedding gown. In Florida, the bridal shops are different than I am used to in the Midwest. The gowns have beads and sequins all covering them; it is hard to tell what the fabric is. When I try them on they seem to be wearing me instead of me wearing the gown. After exhausting all our possibilities, we decide to have a gown custom-made.

There are many other things to do, exciting things. My future in-laws are coming to Florida for a visit and to meet me. They live in upstate NY and I did not meet them when David and I got engaged. They are staying at David's cousin Liz's house. Liz lives in DC part of the year and in Florida the rest of the year.

David wants to be sure my condo is just right before his parents arrive. He asks me if I have an old toothbrush. I ask him why? He says he wants to clean the grout in my bathroom. My condo still feels new to me, but who am I to argue? I find an old toothbrush for David, and marvel at the way he gets on his hands and knees and starts to clean what looks like a clean floor with the toothbrush. At this moment I know I will never have to worry about cleaning floors again. He has set a precedence.

David's parents are lovely people. The first thing I notice is that they are wearing suits, and both of them have the most beautiful white hair, so fancy. They take us out for a dinner and present me with a strand of Mikimoto pearls, fine-quality cultured pearls from Japan, for an engagement gift. What a lovely surprise.

It is interesting that my mother has given me a strand of pearls that my father gave her for their fifth wedding anniversary. I know I will not be able to wear both strands at one time. David has a great solution. Why don't I have my mother's pearls made into a two-strand bracelet, and then I will always be able to wear them together. It is the perfect idea.

David and I spend time registering for our wedding gifts at Bloomingdale's. We pick a Mikasa pattern of stoneware. Not only does the pattern include dinner, salad plates and a teacup and saucer, Mikasa also makes anything else you can think of in the same pattern—serving platters, soup and cereal bowls, coffee mugs, soufflé and covered dishes, a canister set and much more. We have quite a collection when all the gifts arrive. Most of our family and friends send gifts beforehand and every day when I come home from work there is another package at the door. So much fun.

Brent, my future father-in-law, asks me to pick a pattern of Baccarat crystal and he is going to have thirty-six stems sent from France where they are made. It is a very generous gift and one that David and I will treasure.

In late March after having all of the wedding plans in order, David is going to speak at a seminar in Singapore. He asks me to join him on his trip. This will be another first for me, and for David as well. We fly out of the Midwest, so we arrive a couple days early from Florida to visit my family.

Our flight is early in the morning. We arrive at the International Airport and are waiting at the concourse to catch our flight to Hong Kong. We are going there on the way to Singapore. We are onboard ready to go and the flight attendant asks if anyone is willing to give up their seats and take the flight the next morning instead. Northwest will supply the hotel room for the night and give each passenger eight hundred dollars. We look at each other and David says why not!

Now for another adventure, but this time we do not call my relatives and tell them we are in town an extra night. Instead we go straight to the hotel and enjoy the amenities. We swim in the indoor pool, soak in the Jacuzzi and have a relaxing day. We both feel like we are alone on an island and no one knows where we are.

The next morning, we are off to Hong Kong. We have a connecting stop in Narita, Japan. However, the flight takes off late from the airport and we miss our connection to Hong Kong. Northwest put us up in a hotel again, this time in Narita. We get to the hotel and enjoy delicious sushi for dinner and try the next morning to get to Hong Kong.

Our original plans were to spend three days in Hong Kong. When we finally arrive there, it is going to be a short stay, only thirty-six hours. We want to make the most of our time and quickly check into our hotel. We go out for lunch. I am feeling a little woozy and think eating lunch may help. David warns me that I am probably experiencing jet lag. He is right; I have that draggy feeling and am a bit dizzy and very sleepy. Regardless of how I feel we have to see Hong Kong. In the evening the streets are lit up with many neon signs, reminding me of New York City. and now I have a real point of reference since our trip there only three short months ago. The city is loud and busy. We enjoy walking and window shopping. There is something to see in every inch of the city.

We have dinner with a couple that we meet on the plane who are flying back home to Hong Kong. They take us to their favorite restaurant. They insist on ordering and we were glad of that, as the menu is in Chinese. When the food arrives, the first course is prawns. The presentation is rather frightening with the heads of the prawns still on and the feelers still moving and twitching. Plainly I think this is scary. David jumps in and removes the heads and serves me. He is certainly good that way.

That evening I am brushing my teeth, and after I finish I notice a sign under the shelf that is under the mirror in the bathroom. It says, "Don't drink the tap water." Well, I am too late. I ask David what will happen to me and he says that I might get diarrhea. The next morning we are off to Singapore.

*

Arriving in Singapore is so exciting. I know that the city is a safe place to tour by myself. While David is speaking, I tour the city. The water incident follows me to Singapore. The diarrhea only lasts a day and then I am better. We stay at the Holiday Inn Singapore. It is nothing like a Holiday Inn in the United States. It is five stars, with marble everywhere.

I tour the marketplace that has many vendors. They have their wares set up in tent-like areas. It is a small space and they have all of their items filling every corner of the space. I especially enjoy the fresh lychee fruit. And my favorite is the fabric vendor, who has bolts of fabric standing side by side like soldiers on a field. The colors of the fabric are magnificent. Most are silks in every color you can imagine, vibrant solids and many intricate patterns as well.

David and I have dinner every night together, and when he is done speaking at his conference we tour together. We spend a glorious day at the Singapore Botanic Gardens and The Singapore Zoo. We are both animal lovers, and so far every city that we travel to together; it is a must to visit the zoo.

The next morning, we fly back to Florida. We sleep most of the way home and feel good when we get back to my condo. The coming weeks are a whirlwind, getting our wedding invitations in the mail, along with all the remaining details for the wedding.

We pick a banquet hall for our wedding ceremony and reception. Knowing that most of the guests will be coming in from the Midwest, New York and Philadelphia, we decide it will be simpler having one location for everyone to get to. We have a suite of rooms on hold for the guests at the local hotel and transportation will be available as well.

David's friends have a bachelor party for him. He decides to sleep at the apartment that his company provides him the night before the wedding. We do not see each other the night before our wedding ceremony. He calls me in the morning and tells me he has had too much to drink and is going to sleep off the hangover, but promises to put his alarm clock on so he will be at the banquet hall in time for our wedding ceremony.

I ask my nieces Jill and Jennifer to be bridesmaids, and my new niece Sally to be the flower girl. Bonnie, my sister-in-law, is my maid of honor, and David's brother Henry is best man. My nephew Sam, Warren and Bonnie's son, is the ring bearer. The bridesmaids wear fuchsia and all the men wear dark suits. David wears his tux with an ivory shirt, cummerbund and ivory bow tie to match my ivory gown.

My wedding gown is satin with a drop waist and a sweetheart neckline. The bodice of the dress has pearls sewn to it. It has cap sleeves and a long train that flows beautifully when I walk. My veil has a headband that has pearls on it, as well. I don't want anything too high so that I tower over David. The veil is removable, so that I can wear the headband by itself. And the train connects to the bottom of the bodice so that after the ceremony I can walk and dance without tripping.

*

The bridal room is beautiful. My parents arrive and are happy with the venue. It is a bright sunny day and there are chocolate-dipped strawberries on the table. It is Father's Day. Everyone starts to arrive. I greet my future mother-in-law, Jean, and my nieces Jill and Jennifer and new niece Sally. The photographer comes into the bridal suite as well. Everyone looks beautiful in their gowns and I am so happy with how my wedding gown comes out.

I will soon be walking down the aisle. This time I am doing it for keeps. There has been a steep learning curve from my mistakes, and I know deep in my soul that David is the right man to spend the rest of my life with. We are best friends too, which is really the root of any good marriage. I learned that from trial and error.

My friend Debbie helps to line everyone up outside the doors where the ceremony is going to take place. David and the all the male attendants are already in the chapel.

David wanted to get married on the beach with a reggae band. My parents and I are a bit too traditional for that. David always wants to please me, and he agreed that whatever I feel comfortable with will work for him.

First down the aisle is Sally, my flower girl, then Jennifer, Jill and Bonnie. My father walks me halfway down the aisle. He stops, lifts my veil and kisses me on the cheek and we look deeply into each other's eyes. No words are necessary to know how we both feel at that moment. I adore my father.

David walks up the aisle and takes my hand and walks me up the stairs. The ceremony goes quickly after we recited our vows. We kiss and walk back up the aisle, and it feels like walking on air!

At the start of the reception, David's brother Henry and my brother Miles make toasts. We have a videographer to capture these special moments. Our first dance is memorable. The song I choose is "Sweet Love" by Anita Baker. We dance nose to nose staring at each other, and the photographer captures it so beautifully with a silhouette behind us.

The meal is "White Glove French Service." David and I have never seen this type of service before. The chef and at least six of his assistants bring a long, very long, table to the front of the room. There are dinner plates at one end of the table that each server and the chef use to plate the entrée along with the rice pilaf and vegetables—like an assembly line. Once each plate has been filled, servers deliver the plates to the guests. The whole process takes ten minutes to serve the entire room of one hundred and twenty-five people. The meal is delicious, and the food is hot and tasty.

David and I dance the afternoon away; it is magical. We also make sure to visit with all of our relatives and friends. Before we know it the afternoon is over and the guests are getting on the transportation to take them back to the hotel and the airport.

Our wedding night we stay at the airport hotel. We relax and enjoy our first night together as a married couple. We wake up as husband and wife and get ready for our flight to our honeymoon.

*

We had eliminated the idea of going to any island in the middle of June, as the weather is too hot and muggy. By chance I had found an advertisement in a bridal magazine for a resort in Nova Scotia, Canada. I showed it to David and described the place. The resort is right on the ocean, with private cabins. My one criteria is that there is room service in the cabins, and indeed there is. We decide on the wedding package, which includes meals and a week's stay at the resort.

There are many amenities. We are tired and order room service when we arrive at the resort—mussels, French bread and wine. David takes the mussel shells and makes a design out of them…always the artistic one.

We take a basket lunch with lobster rolls out on a canoe along with salad and wine. It is extraordinary, seeing the wildlife and stopping the canoe to enjoy lunch and the still water. There is horseback riding, bike riding, volleyball, shuffleboard, nature trails and so much more.

For some reason the resort is overrun with bunnies. There are dozens of them. They are black and white and very cute. It poses no problem for us, being animal lovers. The bunnies have no desire to enter our cabin, so we are happy as can be to see them when we are outdoors.

*

The week flies by and we return to Florida. I am busy writing thank you notes for our wedding gifts. David and I fly to DC to find a place to live. He will soon be done with his client in Florida and we are moving north. I am so happy. The summers in Florida are oppressive to say the least. I miss the change of seasons and the people.

44

David really wants to live in DC. Being a suburban girl, I am not comfortable with the apartments that have bars on the windows. It is frightening to me and I feel claustrophobic. David suggests we look in Old Towne Alexandria, Virginia, just over the bridge outside of DC.

In just one visit I fall in love with Old Towne Alexandria. David explains that Old Towne, Georgetown and Annapolis, Maryland, were all been built in the 1700s when commerce was brought in by waterways, so all three cities were built near water. We find a wonderful townhouse in Alexandria. It is within walking distance of Old Towne, which is charming and full of history and ethnic restaurants, which we love.

We sign a year lease for the townhouse, knowing that we want to buy a house but are not quite ready for that. The townhouse has three levels. The street level has a kitchen, dining room, living room and powder room. The second floor has two bedrooms and a loft for the third level. It is perfect. I really prefer living in a home that has many levels, always trying to get my workout in.

We fly back to Florida. David is wrapping things up with his client, while I pack our things for the move to Virginia. David asks me to join him in Sacramento, California, for a few days where he has to visit a client. While there, in the evenings, we spend time together. We have lovely dinners out and visit several beautiful lighthouses.

David arranges for us to take a flight to San Francisco to visit a college buddy of his when we are on the west coast. When we are there, he gets a call from his office to come back to DC as soon as possible, as they have a new client for him to visit in Australia. It is a whirlwind. David changes our flights to return to DC instead of Florida. He has to go to Australia as soon as possible. We go to the consulate in DC to get David a visa in order to be able to work there.

Both our passports are in order, so that is not an issue. We then fly back to Florida to complete our packing. David and I are going to have to fly separately to Australia. He has to leave early in January 1991. I have to wait for the movers in Florida, and then fly to our new townhouse in Old Towne Alexandria to meet them before I can fly to Australia to meet David.

So Precious, my cat, and I book a seat together on the plane and meet the movers in Alexandria, VA. I hire a cat sitter in advance to feed and visit daily with Precious while David and I are in Australia. So after being in our new townhouse for less than twenty-four hours, I pack again to leave for Melbourne, Australia. I am not happy about leaving dozens of boxes everywhere, but want to leave as soon as possible because David only has two weeks in Melbourne and I will have barely ten days when I get there.

I fly out of Dulles International Airport in Sterling, Virginia. I sit next to an elderly woman who is a delight. The flight is long, but uneventful. There is one stop in LAX, Los Angeles, California, then on to Australia.

After clearing customs in Melbourne, there is a wide doorway that two or more people can walk through at the same time. You can go left or right out of the doorway. I am not sure why, but I chose to go left. That is a mistake. All I can see is a tour of Asian men and cannot see David anywhere. I even call the hotel in Melbourne to see if he is still there. He finally sees me, and we can't wait to reach each other and hug. It turns out he is standing with the Asian men, but blends in well, being only five foot, eight. We laugh about it.

*

David takes me back to the hotel. We are staying at the Oakford in Melbourne. It is a brand-new hotel. It is very British, and the rooms are exquisite. The bathrooms have wall-to-wall marble. There is a drain on the bathroom floor to allow for the spillover when you use the bathtub. David tells me that Japanese businessmen prefer to bathe that way.

I am only in Australia for a few days when the Gulf War breaks out. Jane Pauley on the *Today* show is reporting it. Things change immediately for David. His company will not allow Americans to fly after the war starts. The original plan is for David to be there for two weeks. His company assigns him more work while we are stuck in Australia for the unforeseen future.

While in Melbourne, I take advantage of the amenities at the hotel. Each morning I swim in the rooftop pool. And during the day I spend most of my time in the Melbourne library, where I am writing a nutritional cookbook.

My business associate and friend, Laura, the dietician continues to encourage me to finish the cookbook I started writing with her a while ago. I still have a shopping bag full of recipes I had created waiting to be published. It is really a labor of love. Writing the book ends up being very time intensive. With a nutrient analysis for each ingredient in each recipe, it is heart healthy, and the American Heart Association is my best customer, ordering cases of books at a time.

On the weekend David and I tour Australia together. In Melbourne, we visit the twelve apostles, magnificent rock stacks that rise up from the Southern Ocean on Victoria's dramatic coastline. They are breathtaking with all the views of the apostles and the ocean surrounding them. What makes it so interesting, as well, is the fact that there are no guardrails along the edges of the mountain ridges overlooking the apostles the way we have in the United States, making me feel freer in nature.

On the recommendation of an aboriginal painter we meet at an art gallery, we visit Wilson Promontory, three hours outside of Melbourne. It is a national park and we are given a map that leads us right to the kangaroos. We park the car and walk across a large clearing where we see dozens of kangaroos.

As we walk, we come across a kangaroo's skull in the dirt. In the distance we can see the kangaroos, even the joeys, the babies in their mom's pouches. We have been instructed to walk very slowly toward them and then stop, as the kangaroos can only see motion. It works well and we get within thirty feet for some fantastic pictures.

We are in Melbourne for two and a half weeks then we fly to Perth. Perth is on the western side of Australia. Even though it is January, it is summertime in Australia. We stay in a small apartment across the water from downtown Perth for the ten days we are there. David and I take the ferry across to the city each morning. It is a beautiful ride, and the waters are so clear you can see the many pink and coral color jellyfish right near the surface.

It turns out to be a glorious trip for both of us. One that is much longer then we planned, but we take total advantage of being halfway around the world from home and being able to see the sites in many cities. We enjoy delicious food. and the Tasmanian salmon is the most memorable. It is plentiful and we love it.

After Perth we fly to Sydney for a couple of days before returning to the States. David is done with his clients and the Gulf War is coming to an end, so his firm is allowing us to fly home. Not having been to Sydney before, it reminds me of San Francisco, with hilly roads and beautiful water views.

We stay in a hotel with views of the harbor. The sunsets are magnificent, and the sunrises are equally beautiful. We tour the city by day and have dinners at an old firehouse that is now a Chinese restaurant. We take advantage of resting up our last night in Australia, knowing that the trip home will be long, and jet lag is likely.

I contact the cat sitter who has been taking care of Precious to let her know we are finally coming home. When we arrive home in Alexandria, I hardly recognize Precious. She is meowing so much she seems to have kitty laryngitis. We also need to unpack our townhouse since I left the day after the movers came. It takes me a full week to unpack and organize everything, but we do settle in nicely.

45

Before I know it, David comes home one day from his DC office and tells me he has a new client in Redding, California, which is in the northern part of the state. We decide to take Precious with us, since David will be there for three months. On the plane, Precious rides anxiously in her pet taxi under my seat. I feel bad for her.

It isn't an easy commute, as we have to take a puddle hopper from San Francisco to Redding. Once we arrive, we stay in a townhouse, similar to the one we are renting in Old Towne Alexandria. We are within walking distance of several restaurants and a megastore Target, a place I have never seen before.

Every Saturday there is a farmer's market that is in the Target parking lot. We get up early and take a long walk and end up at the market to pick up fresh produce. They have many fruits and vegetables that I don't see in our markets at home. Also small yellow and orange tomatoes and patty pans squash, which are in the shape of daisy petals.

We hike in the local area and see beautiful mountains and wildlife. It is a different terrain then the east coast. We are walking in a charming town one Saturday and there is a loud noise coming up the road. It is a Harley Davidson parade with dozens of motorcycles. It goes on for a very long time; we count over 200 Harleys.

When it is time to go home, I am eager to get there and start looking for clients. All of the travel with David has been wonderful, but it is time to start working again.

It has been an amazing year that has already flown by, but it is time to either sign a lease for another year in the townhouse or find an alternative. David and I start searching for houses on the weekends. We look in Alexandria and Arlington, Virginia. What we find are small matchbook homes that were built right after World War II that all look identical. It doesn't matter that they are small, the prices are very high, being close to DC.

David suggests that we take a ride to Annapolis, Maryland, which is about forty-five minutes outside of DC to look for a house. After exiting the highway and driving right into the heart of Annapolis, I must admit, it is love at first sight. The cobblestone streets, the unusual angles that the roads take on, the bayfront stores and all the history. Plus the Naval Academy and all its grandeur.

We park the car and walk into the first real estate office we find. It is on the corner of Main Street. A real estate agent approaches us and asks us what we are looking for in a home. David says we want to find a house on the water, or at least with water views. The agent then asks us what we want to spend and we tell her. She laughs right in our faces. She says we will be lucky to find a water view at the attic level at our price point and that will only be in the wintertime.

She is going to have to eat these words. Betsy is her name and she starts by showing us several houses with a tiny water view. One of the houses has a barking bed. It turns out there is a Schnauzer under the bed who sounds more like an attack dog. David and I spend several weekends looking for houses in Annapolis with Betsy. None of them are right; some are literally cabins on the water with no kitchens and only an outhouse.

Then one Saturday Betsy says she knows of a house that is in a neighborhood close to the Bay Bridge, still Annapolis, but outside of the downtown area. She says the house was recently taken off the market because it does not show well. And she warns me that everything I say I want to stay away from is there. It is a smoker's house and needs a lot of work. It certainly is not turnkey.

Our thinking is changing after hunting for houses for a while and David says let's have an open mind. What the heck! We arrive at the house and drive up the driveway, which leads to the backyard. Or should I say front yard, because when a house is on the water the back yard is really the front yard.

It is a large house, five bedrooms with four levels and two and a half bathrooms. But the house is in ill-repair. The foyer tile is so dirty you cannot see the difference between the grout and the tile. It is shocking when you open the foyer closet door and see how white the grout is. The powder room has outdoor cedar shingles on the walls. The master bedroom is on the fourth level, which is really the attic and has roof lines that slant. The walls have stucco on them and there is a fifth bedroom beyond the master bedroom. The best part is the windows, which look out onto the water. There are two white swans swimming past, majestic and magical at the same time.

On the third level are three bedrooms and a full bathroom. We walk into the first two bedrooms, which both have window seats facing the front of the house, and the third bedroom has a window looking out at the water. When Betsy opens the closet, a ferret comes scurrying out. A teenage boy is in the closet as well, and it is not a walk-in closet. A little strange to say the least. (He and his mother are still living in the house.)

The list goes on of many other "dysfunctions" throughout the house—missing fibers from the living room carpet, a sure sign of some type of insect living in the rugs; rooms with half the wallpaper on and half of it off; and missing hardware and knobs to doors. And the worse and scariest thing is the lowest level, where the powder room is, plus, a family room with wood paneling on the walls and French doors out to the patio. The real killer is the cat door in the laundry room. And the teenage boy tells us that their cat brings in snakes and mice.

We thank Betsy for her time. David and I have dinner in Annapolis and talk about the house. We know that there is another offer on the table. It is a builder who has a contingency and has plans to knock down the house and rebuild on the property, specifically because the lot of land is so beautiful and peaceful with one hundred and twenty five feet of seawall. However, we don't need to include a contingency so we are free as a bird, speaking of which, there are two blue herons that live on the waterway and have been there for over twenty years. So majestic.

David is very happy about the house and its potential. He always has better vision than me. All I can think about is the bad condition the house is in, and that it is a smoker's house. I'm allergic to smoke. David insists that the bad condition is what makes it the perfect opportunity for us and what will enable us to afford the house.

The next morning, we call Betsy with an offer. We spend most of the morning reading over the community bylaws. David finds a real gem in them, the bylaws state that each house must have a two-car garage, and the owner of the home has made the garage into living space. It is a large room with a bay window facing the water. We may use it as a family room.

The current owner accepts our offer. The closing date is set and we meet both real estate brokers at the house for a walk-through. The house is empty so to speak, broom swept. One of the brokers drops a business card with a note on the back saying "it looks like it is a done deal." I see the card on the grass and show it to David. He laughs knowing that we have the cat in the bag as far as the bylaws and the garage issue.

We are at the closing table and we tell our attorney about the bylaws in advance. We know that this is going to be to our advantage. The owner of the house has a down payment on a house in Florida and in order for her to close on it, this house has to close by the end of the day.

David tells Betsy what we discover the missing garage in the community bylaws and that we want to lower our offer in case the community insists on us reconverting the room back to usable garage space. This pushes the owner into a corner and she lowers the price to what we ask.

David's negotiating skills are impressive. He always tells me I am the one with great negotiating skills. I have a collection of art deco pottery, "Red Wing," which was made in Minnesota until the factory closed in 1967. When David and I met, he loved the fact that I have this collection, and together we build it up to a collection of over fifty pieces. David watches me bargain at antique shows and shops for the pottery. He insists this is how he got the skill.

After we sign all the papers, we drive to our new house. I am not ready to call it our home yet. As a matter of fact, we sleep in a tent in the backyard the first night we own the house, because the inside of the house needs so much work. It is late August and luckily the weather is perfect for sleeping outdoors under the moonlight.

*

Since David doesn't do anything halfway and I come from a family that is in the hardware business, we decide we are going take this fixer-upper, gut it and renovate the entire house. I just hope it will not be reminiscent of the movie *The Money Pit* with Tom Hanks and Shelley Long. Saturday morning we start our work. Even though the house is empty at the walk-through, the previous owner has left an assortment of things in the backyard, on the patio and on the deck as well—lawn furniture, a row boat, lawn mowers, other garden equipment, bowling balls, shoes and miscellaneous other items that she no longer wants.

We decide to have a yard sale. We are also going to replace the kitchen appliances and washer and dryer. The salesman at Sears suggests that we advertise the old appliances too. We did not think of this and remarkably we made over a thousand dollars on just the old appliances.

As we decide what we want to do with the interior of the house, we spend many hours making a master plan. First, we are going to do the demolition, pulling up floors, removing walls that are not load-bearing, steaming off wallpaper and pulling out all the tile and fixtures from the three bathrooms.

During our demolition period, David gets a new client in St. Louis, Missouri. He will be there Monday through Friday and come home every weekend. Or I can travel with him and we can both come back to Annapolis together every other weekend. That seems like a better plan and that is what we do. It works out well, as we really did not want to live in the house until the fumigation takes place and the new HVAC system is put in.

So twice a month we fly back home. We accrue many miles on TWA, and get an upgrade to first class because we fly so much and we love that! Shrimp cocktail and white wine.

As the weather gets cooler and we can no longer sleep outside in a tent, we decide to use sleeping bags on the floor in the third bedroom. When we moved out of the townhouse in Old Towne Alexandria, we put most of our things in storage until the house is ready, so we improvise. One Saturday morning I wake with very itchy ankles. My feet have been sticking out of the sleeping bag and I have flea bites. It looks like I have ankle bracelets on.

Our contractors that are installing the HVAC have been complaining of flea bites too. There are fleas living in the carpet, which we soon have ripped out . At that point David remembers he has a queen size blowup bed in storage in Baltimore. He has had all his things there for over two years and we drive there to get the bed. It is much better than sleeping on the floor in sleeping bags.

We are making progress with our work. I take the foyer floor out with a hammer and chisel. When I get down to the wire mesh netting, David helps me pull it out. We have a dumpster for all the debris. We pick out a beautiful cream, white and gray marble tile and David is all ready to install it himself. Again, David does not do anything halfway and he has been studying how to install marble. It is going to be a difficult job.

David's birthday is in January and it is coming up, I suggest that I hire a flooring contractor to install the marble floor for his birthday gift. He thinks it is a great idea. After making that decision, we decide that we can rip apart the house on our own, but need to hire contractors to put it back together. It is a wise and safe choice. This way when David and I are in St. Louis during the week, we give a key to the contractors and they can do their work while we are away, and we meet up with them on the weekends.

*

Life is different in St. Louis. The first few nights we stay at a hotel in downtown St. Louis, which was originally a YMCA. I am eager to find us an apartment. We will only have one car, so David suggests we find a place within walking distance of his client. That means living downtown. Now don't worry, it isn't a downtown like New York, Chicago or Hong Kong. It is a downtown where the city rolls up at night.

I want to get back to my healthcare consulting, so I contact medical professionals in the area and am lucky to meet Sue West. She is a professional coder for doctors of all specialties. She feels that my expertise complements hers and she is happy to refer me to some of her clients.

Sue and I take a ride to Farmington, Missouri, outside of St. Louis, about a forty-minute drive each way. She introduces me to Dr. Williams, a doctor whose wife has been running his practice, and now wants to stay at home and raise their children. The office is still on a ledger card system and is very behind in their accounts receivable.

It is the perfect fit for me. I will be converting their paper systems to a computer system and training the staff how to use it. I will be working there three days a week, indefinitely. Dr. Williams is aware that I am living in St. Louis for a year's time, and feels confident, as do I, that his practice will be running smoothly before I leave.

46

David and I want to start a family. I discuss it in length with Carl that I will need to titrate off the lithium before trying to get pregnant. Even though I am now on a lower dose of the medication, it isn't going to be safe to be on it while pregnant, especially the first trimester.

David is very patient and knows that it is going to be scary for me to go off the lithium. We both think that doing consulting work and managing the contractors at our house in Annapolis, mostly long distance, is enough to do. Though concentrating on getting ready to start a family is certainly a priority as well.

I keep in close contact by phone with Carl. After two weeks of cutting the lithium back, I become apprehensive and nervous about being without it. I just don't feel it is the right time after all. I discuss it with David and we decide to wait until we return to Annapolis.

During our stay in St. Louis, David and I tour the area on the weekends that we spend there. One of our first outings is to the Gateway Arch on St. Louis' river front. There is a tram inside the arch. We wait in line for over forty-five minutes to enter the elevator, which has the tram inside. You can ride the tram up inside the arch and look out at St. Louis from tiny windows at the top of the arch.

The tram is egg-shaped and the compartments have a ceiling that slopes. It is very close quarters. I have no idea how close until we are near the head of the line and I can see the inside of the tram. I start to sweat. I know that I am claustrophobic, and this is not going to be easy for me. I whisper in David's ear that I don't think I can do it. He insists I will be OK and he will hold my hand the whole time. I suggest that he go by himself and I will wait outside for him. He isn't happy with this idea and we both walk out of the line.

David has this idea that holding my hand and being with me solves all my problems. It is a lovely thought, but not always practical. Earlier during our stay in St. Louis, we went to the zoo. The St. Louis Zoo came about after the World's Fair was held there in 1904.

There is a reptile house at the St. Louis Zoo. I inherit a snake phobia from my mother, who said she had a horrible dream about snakes as a kid and subsequently was afraid of snakes. She had my father cut out any pictures in the newspaper, etc. of snakes, before she would read them. It is hard not to be afraid, as she made such a big deal about snakes.

On our visit to the zoo, I told David I could skip the reptile house. Once again, he suggested facing my fears and that I could hold his hand as we walk through the reptile house and he promised not to spook me or play any games. I decided to take the plunge. Of course, all the reptiles are behind glass and David is great about it. I must say that it was a success for me, and to this day, snakes don't bother me the way they did. Not that I will be the one holding the boa constrictor at an animal show.

*

The weeks and months go by and we enjoy our stay in St. Louis as the renovations on our new home in Annapolis continue. After a year we say our good-byes to our clients and leave St. Louis. David isn't sure where his next client will be, so he takes a couple of weeks' vacation to work on the house when we get back home.

Things are coming along nicely. David designs a wall unit in the living room for our Red Wing pottery. All the floors have been done, in the kitchen, bathrooms and foyer. And all the carpeting is new.

I spend time with contractors trying to figure out how to fix the master bedroom walls. They all want to add sheetrock to cover the stucco on the walls and I do not want to make the room smaller in anyway. Instead, I fill a spray bottle with water and spray the walls to loosen up the stucco material, and use a spackle knife to remove the stucco. It is a long tedious process, but finally

I finish. Then David paints the room, along with all the other walls in the house. He even buffs out and refinishes the hardwood floors in the family room. We stay at a local hotel the night he refinishes the floors so as not be near or inhaling the dangerous fumes.

We continue to work on the house, mostly on the weekends. I create a new brochure and purchase a mailing list from the County Medical Association and send out one hundred flyers. I visit the offices where I have sent flyers, and on my second day find a new client, Leonard Alter, MD, a psychiatrist in a medical office building about twenty minutes from home.

47

David is traveling and I am working on building my consulting business. I am doing consulting work at Leonard Atler's office working with his manager. It is my second month there and I observe patients with all sorts of problems: depression, OCD, mania, along with other mental illnesses. The patient that Leonard is seeing that day rushes out of his office and out the door. Leonard tells us that he has pushed the emergency button under his desk, which goes directly to the police station. Leonard warns us that the patient says he is going down to his car to get a gun.

Leonard's office is on the fourth floor of the medical building and Kelsey, his office manager, and I decide to hide in the bathroom, which has a steel door and a lock. We don't feel there is time to go down the steps or take the elevator, in case we run into the angry patient.

Kelsey and I stay in the bathroom for thirty minutes. Leonard has left the office and goes into one of the other offices on the fourth floor to watch for the police from the window. According to Leonard they arrive quickly and there are three squad cars with six police officers. They are able to catch the man with the gun and take him to the station. Later, after we are all safe again, Leonard tells us that the patient had been in a car accident and has a brain injury, which may be why he loses control.

*

I see my OB/GYN for a yearly checkup and he tells me my blood pressure is high. It is higher than he likes and wants me to keep an eye on it. A week or so later I wake up with a bad headache, David is away. I shower and get ready to visit my new client, Joseph Vanders, MD. When I arrive at his office, I ask him if he does not mind taking my blood pressure. The reading is 160/110 and he advises me to see my doctor immediately.

I go see my internist, Dave Gold, MD. Dr. Gold is stumped. He takes my blood pressure several times from my left arm and then pulls out a very large cuff that is meant to fit over your thigh. I have never seen anything like it. It is frightening, even as he explains that he just wants to verify that my blood pressure is the same as when he takes it the more conventional way.

The highest reading he gets is 150/105, and tells me I have to go to the hospital immediately. He says he will call an ambulance, but I tell him I am OK to drive since it is only five minutes from his office. I drive directly there and he admits me to the critical care unit. The nurse starts an IV to bring down my blood pressure. I tell her I am having cramping and a very heavy period. When I use the bathroom I am experiencing stomach pain and I see clots of blood in the toilet. She asks if I might be pregnant. David and I have been trying and I don't know if I am pregnant or not. The clots keep coming and it becomes clear that the very high blood pressure causes a miscarriage.

I call David who is at his clients in Chicago and he takes the next flight home. By the time he reaches the hospital the IV has brought down my blood pressure. Now that it is down. the doctor moves me to a regular hospital room. I no longer need to be in the critical care unit. I am glad David does not see me there. It is a scary place, with small cubical-like rooms and lots of large windows instead of walls, so that the nurses can see the patients from the nursing station. And most of the patients are semiconscious. It might have frightened David.

Dr. Gold orders a consultation with John Carson, MD, a nephrologist, to check me out. David is with me when Dr. Carson comes into my hospital room. He tells us how excited he is to have a young patient like me, who must have a kidney blockage that is causing the high blood pressure. At this point, I don't know how much of my history he knows, but he is positive that he is right about the blockage. He wants to schedule an arteriogram, where they stick a small tube somewhere near the kidney to see if the fluids are moving properly or not.

David and I know this can be a very dangerous test, because a lot can go wrong, but both my doctors feel it is necessary. I have the test the next day. David is able to stay with me and sits by the gurney and holds my hand the whole time. His strength is such a gift. He never wavers and he is always there for me. That evening when Dr. Carson walks into the room, Dr. Gold is there as well for evening rounds. Dr. Carson says "oops" and announces that there is no blockage. He is stumped and has no idea what to do with me and is signing off the case. We are also stumped. Since when does a doctor just sign off the case like that?

Dr. Gold says my case is too complex to stay at the local hospital and it will be best if I see a different nephrologist at Johns Hopkins in Baltimore. He refers me to Patterson Russ, MD. I have a two-hour consultation with Dr. Russ; it always takes me a while to go through my history. He tells me that I will need a series of tests before he can determine which medication he will prescribe that will be safe during a pregnancy. Dr. Gold had prescribed Zestril, to lower the blood pressure after leaving the hospital. Zestril is an ace-inhibitor, which works through the kidneys. However, Dr. Russ informs me that Zestril is a teratogenic, which can disturb the growth and development of an embryo or fetus and will not be safe to take during pregnancy.

Dr. Russ suggests a diuretic instead of the Zestril, along with a list of blood tests and a kidney test to determine how much function I have in each kidney. That test is not difficult. I have to lie still on a narrow table while they inject me with dye and take pictures and measurements of the kidney. The test is easy enough, but the results are far more painful. Dr. Russ tells me that half of my kidney function is gone and that I have *renal insufficiency*. He believes it is from the lithium toxicity I had as a teenager. I have permanent organ damage. Taking all this in is difficult. This is far worse than the bladder failure I had when I was 23 years old. That was temporary, this is permanent. The anger comes to the top again. What were my parents thinking?

It seems the best way to protect myself is to learn everything I can about renal insufficiency and pull back into my shell; that is, not be in denial about what is going on, but try to separate myself from the magnitude of the problem. It all comes back to me how disgusting the decisions my mother made over the years and her constant betrayal, poisoning me little by little.

It takes almost a year for Dr. Russ to find the right medication to control my high blood pressure, so that it will be safe for me to get pregnant again. He keeps raising the dose of the diuretic and it does not work. Finally, he tries Lopressor, which is a beta blocker. It works, but also adds ten pounds to my weight in the first two weeks I am on it. I am willing to sacrifice in order to have a baby. Dr. Russ is my lifeline. While I am waiting for the right medication to take hold, I have an appointment with a high-risk OB/GYN, Hal Gordon, MD, at Johns Hopkins. Dr. Gordon asks about my medical history, and once again I have to relive it, a stressful process to say the least. He shakes his head in a negative way, as if to say no way. He tells me that if I get pregnant again, I will never be able to carry to term. I will die.

*

After my consultation with Dr. Gordon, I walk out of his office in a daze and out of Johns Hopkins. There is an old, scary-looking church right next door. I walk in and fall to my knees and start to pray. There is no one around to talk to except God. That has always been good enough in the past and it is good enough right now. After begging God for help, praying and promising to do whatever it takes to give David a baby, I pull myself together and drive home. During the ride home, I am planning what to do next. The minute I walk through the door, I call Dr. Russ and tell him what Dr. Gordon has said, about dying if I get pregnant. Dr. Russ is an older man who is kind and gentle and he tells me that he thinks I should see another high-risk OB/GYN and not dwell on Dr. Gordon's comments. Easy to say, harder to do.

I make an appointment to see Jean Cullen, MD, also at Johns Hopkins. Again, going through my medical history, she has some optimistic things to share with me. She says it will be a very high-risk pregnancy, she is willing to take me on as a patient, but first she wants me to see a urologist to see if my bladder is strong enough for a pregnancy. I see James Moss, MD, and once again go through my medical history. Dr. Moss tells me that my bladder is strong enough to hold a baby during pregnancy, but most likely I will need to learn to insert a catheter in my bladder to be sure it is empty, during my third trimester.

On my way home, I think about all the sacrifices I can make to give David a baby. My parents are visiting from the Midwest that week and they are having a late breakfast when I walk in my house. I explain to them what Dr. Moss has told me about the catheter, etc. My mom doesn't say much, and my father says, as he is looking out the window, what a beautiful day it is. As strange as this may seem, this is his way, denial. He does not want to admit to the many poor decisions they have made regarding my health throughout the years. In addition to the unneeded psychiatric commitments, there were the steroids that were so wrong and only put a band aid on the problem, the lithium that was prescribed and not needed. So many medical issues could have been avoided if they had only thought more about the consequences of their decisions. They were responsible for leaving my body with permanent damage and the uncertainty of ever having children.

Soon after, David tells me that he has a new client in Alabama. It is to be a three-year assignment and the firm will allow us to fly back and forth together every other weekend, instead of David flying back there each Monday and returning home Friday and us being apart all week. With my consulting work, it is easy for me to travel to new cities with David. My clients at home in the Annapolis area are doing fine and they agree to FedEx me documents that I need to work on, etc. However, at this time, I won't be looking for new clients in Alabama. Instead I will concentrate on finding a new high-risk OB/GYN and having a healthy baby.

48

Life was so good for me and David, except for a tragedy in his family. About six months earlier, we had been at a family gathering in Rochester, where David was born and his parents currently live during their retirement. David's brother Henry is there with his wife Cathy. Cathy is coughing a lot and using an inhaler. This does not seem like a good sign. Soon after, we find out that Cathy is going into the hospital for tests and treatment. A few months later Cathy dies at 49 years old; such a sad time. We drive to New York for the funeral and stay with David's family for a few days. It is hard to know what to do at this time, except to be there. Cathy was so young.

*

David and I are in the process of renovating our home in Annapolis and work on it the weekends we are home. Then the contractors come in when we are away in Alabama during the week. It really is a great plan. Who needs to be around when contractors are making all kinds of noise and dust?

I am lucky enough to meet a young woman in Alabama whose husband is a doctor. She asks him who he recommends as a high-risk OB/GYN for me and he sends me to a group of thirteen doctors. Edward Frank, MD, is the one to see. This group is part of a teaching hospital, which is a good thing. The consultation goes well. Dr. Frank tells me in no uncertain terms that every woman should be able to have one baby. He says to go home and get pregnant. Getting pregnant is not the issue; having the baby full term is.

It is Valentine's Day, February 14, 1994 almost 2 years since the miscarriage. David and I are home in Annapolis for the weekend. We make love, and afterwards, I put my legs on two pillows, leaving them high up in the air for fifteen minutes. Many women who have had girls tell me about this trick.

Next month I miss my period and immediately make an appointment with Dr. Frank. He does a blood test on the spot and tells me that I am indeed pregnant. I have total faith in Dr. Frank; I have to trust someone. And whether or not to trust doctors has been an issue for me for such a long time. I go with my instincts. Dr. Frank has been direct, kind and understanding from the start. He tells me I will have to see him every week until week thirty of my pregnancy, and twice a week after that, unless I deliver early. He also tells me that he will be there for the delivery and that I won't rotate seeing other doctors for my visits. I will strictly see him. I am totally compliant; my life is in his hands.

I am over the moon! I don't know what to do first. I can call David at work, but I want to tell him face to face and see his expression. It is already late in the afternoon and David will be home in a few hours. I get busy preparing dinner and listen for his key in the door. We are living in a cute two-bedroom townhouse, right on a lake. David walks in and I run to him. I don't need to say a word. He knows instantly we are having a baby.

I share all the details with David. Dr. Frank has also given me many other instructions, I have a list. At week twenty I am no longer going to be able to fly home and will be housebound, except for my visits to see him. Not wanting to rock the boat or step out of any lines that Dr. Frank has drawn, I take a chance and ask him if I can possibly go out with David for lunch on Saturdays, as we do not have any family in Alabama and I will need that time with David to get the nursery ready, etc. He agrees.

Dr. Frank also tells me it is likely that I may have preeclampsia, a condition that can occur during pregnancy after week twenty that causes very high blood pressure. Another name for it is toxemia, and I might need to deliver early. He is especially going to watch my high blood pressure. He says that it is possible that I will carry the baby to week thirty and then have a C-section and the baby will be in the neonatal unit. None of this would be necessary if my mother thought of the consequences of her actions instead of only thinking about herself.

He also suggests I have an amniocentesis because I am 36 years old. The test is usually done between weeks fifteen and eighteen, to rule out certain birth defects, which there is a higher risk of the older the mother is. Paul Snow, MD, is part of Dr. Frank's group and is the one who does the amniocentesis. During the procedure, I ask Dr. Snow to explain what he is doing. He says that he is going to insert a large needle, about three and one-half inches long into my belly to extract a small amount of amniotic fluid, which they will send to pathology. I notice that the fluid he is extracting is a yellow color. I ask him why it isn't blue for a boy, or pink for a girl. Dr. Snow tells me that none of his other patients have ever said anything funny during the procedure!

It takes about two weeks to get the results of the amniocentesis. I am standing looking out at the water in our townhouse when Dr. Frank calls. It is about ten in the morning and he is happy to report that my results are all normal. He asks me if I want to know the gender of the baby. I really want it to be a surprise, but David encourages me to get as much information as possible; he always says knowledge is power. "Yes," and Dr. Frank, tells me we are having a girl! This is exactly what I want to hear. The legs in the air did the trick! After growing up in a house with three brothers, I am yearning for a girl. I will be the right kind of mother, loving and caring, always there for our child—not self-absorbed, mean and cold.

Since it is such a high-risk pregnancy, we decide not to tell anyone that we are having a girl. That means family and friends as well. When I go for my visits to Dr. Frank, strangers walk up to me and tell me I am having a girl. They say I am carrying mostly in front and that is a true sign. Right after the amnio results, Dr. Frank schedules a fetal echocardiogram. He says I need that because I am on lithium—a lesser dose then when my mother convinced Dr. Synder to raise the dose, but still potentially harmful, which can cause a heart problem to the fetus. Thankfully, I pass this test as well. If there is something wrong with her heart, David and I will have to make a decision as to whether or not to continue the pregnancy or abort it. Fortunately, we do not have to make that decision.

Since I am no longer able to fly home to Annapolis, David and I spend our weekends decorating the nursery. We pick out a beautiful white crib and changing table, along with a twin bed for the nursery, in case one of us needs to sleep in the baby's room.

David enjoys drawing and starts sketching a lamb. It evolves into a fuzzy-looking lamb standing and smiling at me. He names it "ShuShu the Lamipoo." David makes stencils of ShuShu and a stencil of a very feminine bow. He paints a pink border in the baby's room alternating ShuShu and the bow. It is adorable. After we finish decorating with linens for the bed and crib, in soft pink and white strips, along with bumpers and a mobile with Beatrix Potter animals, I often go into the nursery and read on the bed while I am waiting for our baby to come.

At week thirty, David and I visit the neonatal unit as Dr. Frank suggests. It is miraculous to know that in this place modern medicine can help so many tiny babies that may have been born early, etc. But it is a scary place too, seeing the babies on monitors and with air tubes in their noses. We pray our baby will not need this unit. Also at the beginning of week thirty, Dr. Frank starts seeing me for checkups twice a week, and once a week I have a non-stress test. This is a painless procedure to evaluate the baby's condition. The technician checks for the baby's heartbeat, while the baby is resting and while the baby is moving. The test is often done when you have a high-risk pregnancy. Dr. Frank also says to make sure to tell him if I notice the baby isn't moving every so often. This is another call I do not need to make.

I tell Dr. Frank that David's client he is working for wants to have a surprise baby shower for him. This is a new concept to me, a baby shower for the expectant father. Being compliant and homebound at this time, I ask for special permission to attend the baby shower. Dr. Frank agrees, as long as I don't drive there myself. The expression on David's face is priceless when he walks into the room; he turns bright red. There are wonderful baby gifts and a pack' n play portable crib too. They serve lunch and a beautiful cake as well. It is so generous and caring of all of them to do this for David and me.

At week thirty-six, Dr. Frank tells me his plan for my delivery. He is very happy the way things are progressing. He tells me if I haven't had the baby by week thirty-nine, his plan is to induce me three times. It will be a Tuesday, Thursday and Saturday night. If I do not dilate enough to have the baby naturally by Saturday, he will do a C-section. He wants me to have a very short labor, which is why he is planning the three inductions.

David takes me to the hospital Tuesday at 5 p.m. They put an IV in to give me the medication to start inducing my labor. David stays by my bedside the whole night. The doctor tells me if nothing happens I will come back Thursday. David and I are both up most of the night. Dr. Frank checks me the next morning, and tells us to go home because the induction has not done its job yet.

David showers and goes off to work. I stay on the couch all day listening to harp music, which is very relaxing for me and the baby. I am sixty-four pounds heavier with the pregnancy and am very ready to have the baby. Thursday night at 5 p.m., David takes me back to the hospital again. Dr. Frank examines me and tells us my cervix is 1 centimeter and that they are going to start the IV again. At 6 a.m. the next morning they will break my water and give me an epidural. Hopefully I will be ready to give birth vaginally.

That night David holds my hand and will not let go. What an incredible man. I always feel safe with him near me. It is almost as if the world stops and we are the only two people in it. Friday 6 a.m. comes and Dr. Snow, who did my amniocentesis, comes to examine me and tells me that I am over 6 centimeters and that he is going to break my water. After that, he inserts the needle for the epidural and tells us the labor nurse will stay with me until they need Dr. Frank. I have a very easy labor. I push on three different occasions and the nurse says the baby is coming fast and she will find Dr. Frank immediately. Dr. Frank walks in the room at 8:20

a.m. It is the same room I have been in since the night before. It is a pleasant room, with a large window with natural light coming in and plenty of room for all the equipment and professionals.

When the next labor pain comes, Dr. Frank says to push a little harder. David is sitting on a stool feeding me ice chips and keeping his eyes on my face. I don't think he wants to look beyond the stirrups. I tell Dr. Frank it hurts a lot that time, and he says that is because the baby's shoulders have just come out, and with one more big push the baby will be born.

Friday 8:40 a.m., November 16, 1994, I make the big push and the baby is born. Dr. Frank holds her up in the air and then rests her on my tummy. He cuts the umbilical cord, ties it off and hands the nurse our baby. She is crying and David walks over to get a closer look. The first thing he says is, "she has your 'curly toe'." It is a trait going back to my maternal grandmother. The second toe next to the baby toe on each foot curls in towards the other toes.

We have a name for our baby girl, Kate Paige. Kate is a name we have fallen in love with. We want to name her after my two grandmothers Fran and Paula, but instead decide on Kate in memory of David's sister-in-law, his brother Henry's wife, who went by Cathy, and her given name was Katherine.

Kate is a joy! She weighs six pounds, eleven ounces and I am afraid to bathe her; she seems like a small, fragile chicken to me. We have a baby bathtub that fits over the double sink in the kitchen and David often bathes her, and keeps telling me not to worry, she isn't going to break. When Kate is six weeks old, we begin to travel back and forth again to Annapolis. David carries Kate in the baby holder that wraps around him, with her head bobbing near his face. When we get home, he loves to rock her to sleep to Steve Winwood CDs.

I spend a lot of time calling friends and relatives, even though we send out baby announcements that are in the shape of ShuShu with a pink ribbon. I cannot wait to call Susan; she had visited during my second trimester. Susan was originally from Alabama, and had taken the bus from the Midwest to visit and care for me while I was pregnant with Kate.

When she came to visit us, David picked her up at the train station and she stayed with us for a few days. She insisted on making her famous apple pie for us. We thoroughly enjoyed each other's company and caught up on so many things. I am so lucky to have Susan in my life. I don't want to think where I would be without her.

Kate is a happy baby, she coos and smiles and especially loves to sleep in her battery-operated swing. The best part of that is she often naps in it for three to four hours, while I am working at the dining room table, looking up at her and thinking she looks like a porcelain doll.

When Kate can sit up on her own, she loves going on errands with me, especially to the grocery store. She smiles at all the people as we pass them. I am not able to put my finger on it, but it seems to me she is not only very friendly, but born intuitive.

At one of my follow-up visits with Dr. Frank, he tells me how glad he is that my pregnancy went so well, and that he thinks David and I can try to get pregnant again. My first reaction is to tell him he and David can get pregnant and leave me out of it. I have a healthy baby and managed to get though the pregnancy without many problems. I go home and discuss it with David. He thinks it is a great idea. Since we will be living in Alabama for another year, why not try to have another baby?

We wait until Kate is seven months old, and I am pregnant after one try. Things are moving along nicely. Dr. Frank and David are very happy. I feel uneasy. At week eleven I call Dr. Frank and tell him something doesn't seem right. He asks me to come to the office to have a vaginal ultrasound to see how the fetus is doing. He is there during the test and shows me on the monitor that he cannot find the fetus. Dr. Frank says not to worry. It can be hiding, and I need to lay low and come back in a week for another ultrasound. When I return for the test, there is evidence that the fetus is no longer developing, and he says I am having a miscarriage, a blighted ovum and need to have a D&C.

He wants to schedule it for the next day. Unfortunately, David is going to be away for that day on business and it is too late for him to cancel, which is unfortunate, but I totally understand. Dr. Frank says the procedure can wait a couple of days, but he is also going to be out of town as well and another doctor in his group will have to do it. After thinking it over, I prefer to have Dr. Frank do the D&C, and I call a friend who can pick me up at the hospital when I am ready to go home. David is able to drop me off at the hospital on his way out of town.

When Kate was born, we had hired an aide, Anne, to help me with Kate when I first came home from the hospital. She would come at 7 p.m. and stay for twelve hours the first two weeks we are home. That way David and I could get a good night's sleep. After interviewing several people for the job, she reminded me of Susan, and Anne came onboard. After I no longer need help in the evenings, Anne stayed on to help when I started working again. I have a client that is opening a pain and wellness clinic. I do consulting work for him two to three days a week. I give Anne a call. I tell her about the miscarriage, and she asks if I need her to take care of Kate and she arranges to be there for me.

I am waiting in a cubicle at the outpatient surgery department at the hospital with my two hospital gowns on, one that ties in the front and one that ties in the back. The anesthesiologist comes into the room after the nurse starts an IV. He tells me he wants to put some medication in the line that will help me relax. I mention my renal insufficiency and ask him to give me a smaller dose, since my kidneys take longer to filter the medication than someone with normal kidney function. He looks at me as if I have two heads and says, "Don't worry about it." I ask him if Dr. Frank is there yet and he says no. I then ask him if he can wait until Dr. Frank comes, because he says I am going to be awake during the D&C. He tells me curtly that is not possible, and he proceeds to put the medication in my IV anyway.

I force myself to stay alert and focus so that I will be awake and coherent when Dr. Frank finally arrives. I am having difficulty and am nodding off. Dr. Frank sees that I am trying to communicate to him. He is holding my hand and I recognize him, but at this point I am unable to speak and cannot get my point across. Someone then wheels me into the surgical room and I don't remember anything else until I wake up in recovery on a gurney. After I become more alert, my friend Ellen is able to take me home.

Dr. Frank tells me I might have some bleeding and that is normal, to rest for the next couple of days and see him in his office the following week. Anne is feeding Kate when I get home. She asks me how I am doing and I tell her it went well, except for the anesthesiologist, who is unkind to say the least.

The next morning when I wake up. my neck is bothering me. I look in the mirror and see that I have bruises from under my chin down my whole neck. When the anesthesiologist intubated me prior to the D&C, it seems obvious that he was too rough. David is very upset when he sees my neck. I know I can call the state and report the doctor, but I have better things to do. I need to recover mentally from losing the baby, even though it is so early in my pregnancy. This is so sad for us. We want Kate to have a sibling, and having another baby while under Dr. Frank's care is so important to my health care. But this is the way life is.

*

Our time in Alabama comes to an end and we pack up to return to Annapolis. David drives the U-Haul with all the furniture and clothes. I drive my car home and David follows us the whole way. Kate is eighteen months, and it is interesting trying to entertain her with singing, etc., while I am driving. Kate loves to pull her shoes and socks off every time she is in her car seat. She giggles and throws them all over the back seat.

After we settle back in Annapolis, I contact my clients and return to work part-time. I interview several people to stay with Kate and visit a few family day care homes as well. I decide to leave Kate at a family daycare where she will be able to socialize. She thrives there and loves being with the kids. She is like a little monkey as Ms. Laura takes the kids twice a week to an indoor playground with lots to climb on.

49

David is still traveling for work and comes home on the weekends. He tells me he has a new assignment in Hong Kong, to make sure my passport is up to date and get a passport for Kate. We will be in Hong Kong for a year. It is a turbulent time in Hong Kong, because in 1997 Hong Kong is reverting back to China, as it has been under British rule from 1842 to 1997.

Before leaving for Hong Kong, David has a convention in Atlanta, where he runs into an old business associate who is forming a start-up firm in New England. He offers David the position as Senior Vice President of Strategic Planning and he asks him to think it over for a few days and get back to him. There isn't much for me to think over; it sounds like a great career opportunity and we will not have to leave the states. David gives notice to his office in DC, and we start packing for New England.

I really don't like the cold weather, and after being away from the Midwest for many years, I know it will be an adjustment. We visit New England to find a place to live and we put our house up for sale. It is funny how things happen. The renovations on our Annapolis home are now complete, and we love the way it looks. Besides the mild climate and my clients, I have not been able to find time to make many friends in the five years we have owned the house, with being in Alabama for three of those years. Now off to another adventure.

We end up renting a townhouse while we look for a house. It is different and difficult. New England is like a new world to me. I am looking for neighborhoods and my point of reference for that is from the Midwest and what my subdivision was like growing up. New England is nothing like that. First of all, the houses are not brick. They have clapboards, a form of siding on the outside walls, and the paint or stain is all different colors. Nothing seems to fit; there might be a large colonial and a tiny house next to it, very eclectic.

The people are even worse. I often speak with people in the grocery line here, they don't! I get looks like I am speaking another language. And making friends, well talk about a challenge, many of the people I meet have been in New England forever and are fifth, sixth and seventh generation or more, with big families, and not looking for new friends.

After searching for nine months we find a house that is only six years old, very unusual to find newer construction in this area. It is a nice house, and the best part is that the washer and dryer are on the second floor. We will end up living there for two years and are able to enjoy the beach, yes the ocean, which is a mile from our house. It is purely a slice of heaven, considering how long the winters are. I can tell you for sure that there are only three seasons in New England winter, summer and a glorious fall.

*

We find a wonderful preschool for Kate and I often take her there in a racing stroller. When I pick her up one afternoon, we get home and Precious, who is 13 years old, is howling in the master bedroom, hiding under a chair in the corner. She has not been herself the last few days, hiding in the closet in our room. We think she is just trying to become familiar with the new surroundings. I do not have a new vet yet and it is already 5 p.m. I look in the local phone book and find a vet nearby. His office is closed, but the recording says Dr. Lambert is covering for him. I call Dr. Lambert and tell him about Precious and he says to bring her right in. Kate and I put a towel in a basket and gently lift Precious onto it. We have to drive twenty minutes to the next town. Dr. Lambert examines her and takes x-rays. He tells me he isn't sure what is wrong, but wants to keep her overnight and will call me in the morning. Kate and I go home; Kate is sad and we both worry about Precious.

Dr. Lambert calls the next morning; it is February, a Friday morning. He tells me that Precious has had an aneurism, which is why her back legs and tail are not moving normally. He tells me that I have two choices. I can take her to an animal hospital, or I can put her down. I am having a difficult time processing all of this. It is clear that Precious may not recover and I have to make a decision. I ask Dr. Lambert what he thinks. He says he feels it is more humane to put her down, as he isn't sure they can reverse the damage that the aneurism caused. I agree that putting her down will be best for her. I don't want her to be in pain anymore and taking her to a hospital where she will not know anyone will be unthinkable at this point. Dr. Lambert tells me that he wants me to come to his office at noon to say good-bye to Precious.

David is at work and Kate is at preschool. I first call my friend Jessica to see if she is available to drive me to the vet, since I am in no condition to drive myself. I then get on the phone and call the Humane Society and animal shelters to find two kittens. I want to be able to tell Precious that I am going to adopt two kittens, because she has given me so much unconditional love.

It is not an easy job, finding kittens in February. None of the shelters that I call have any kittens. Finally I find one that recommends a woman who has several kittens she is trying to find homes for. I call her at once and she says she has three kittens left from the litter of six. I tell her my circumstances and that I will not be able to pick up the two kittens until the next day, Saturday. She says that is fine and I can pick from the three kittens that are left.

Jessica picks me up and takes me to Dr. Lambert's office to say good-bye to Precious. Precious perks up when she hears my voice and I go over to her and start petting her head. She begins purring and I begin to cry. I tell her to never forget what a wonderful pet, friend and companion she has been. And that I have found two kittens that will be her legacy. For the last time I kiss her forehead and leave the room. I cry the whole way home.

The next morning, David, Kate and I are on our way to pick up the kittens. The lady we are adopting the kittens from says they are free. We can't decide what to bring her and end up stopping at the local bakery to pick up fresh bread. We get to her house and there are only two kittens left. The third kitten finds a home before we get there. I am glad, so that we do not have to choose. The kittens are only six weeks old; so tiny that they fit right in the palm of your hand. I take the kittens sight unseen and have no idea what they look like. Amazing but true, one is a tuxedo cat, just like Precious; her markings are very similar. And the other kitten is very dark brown, almost black, with a spot of white fur on the belly. We thank the woman again and again and put both kittens in Precious' pet taxi.

The kittens are so tiny we have no idea what gender they are. We have an appointment with the vet and he informs us that the one that looks just like Precious is a girl and the brown/black one with the white spot on his belly is a boy. We thank Dr. Lambert for all his kindness with Precious and helping us with the new kittens.

Once again we use a name that my brother Warren used for one of his cats. We name the tuxedo cat Squeakey, as she squeaks when she meows. The other kitten has a lot of brown in his fur, especially when you look at him in the sunlight, and we name him Minkey. Everyone grieves differently and some of my friends wait weeks before bringing a new pet into their homes. That isn't for me. I wanted the kittens right away, especially to be able to tell Precious about them before she went to kitty heaven. David likes to kid me that when he goes, I will replace him with two twenty-year-old men. Hardly!!

50

Now that we are settled in New England, there is only one thing to do—and I know that adopting a child is the way to go, especially since David is adopted. What an exceptional gift to give him. I knew that after my last miscarriage I could not risk going through another pregnancy. I made the decision to have my tubes tied. David was respectful and knew it was my decision. He made it crystal clear that he wasn't having a vasectomy. He wanted no change to his favorite appendage, and I in turn was respectful of that.

My first call is to Julie, my sister-in-law Lois's sister, who is raising two girls they found through an adoption agency in Texas. Texas is one of the only states that has the birth mother sign off the day the adoptive parents pick up the baby. All other states give the birth mother six months to change her mind and rip the baby out of the adoptive parents' arms. That is not an option for us. We will consider an international adoption if we cannot adopt in Texas.

I call the agency and speak with the director. We want to be gender-specific; we are asking for a boy. She says there is no problem accommodating our wishes, as most people want to adopt girls.

The agency asks us to assemble three family picture albums, which need to have pictures of David and me when we are babies, our wedding photos and some family pictures including Kate. I make three identical albums, which also require a Dear Birth Mommy letter. David writes the letter:

Dear Birth Mommy,

We are very excited about this wonderful opportunity to add to our family. Without you this could not be possible. Your child will be raised with love and affection and will have an older sister with which to play and grow. We have a large home, which is full of warmth and opportunities for learning and growing in a safe environment.

Since David is adopted, we believe that we will have a unique relationship with our new child. David believes that he will have a very special bond with a child that is just like him! And I know I have plenty of love in my heart for another child to complete our family.

We believe that education is a very important part of growing up. David and I were fortunate to go to undergraduate school, and he attended graduate school as well. We will give the same opportunities to all our children.

This child will be surrounded with family, friends and all that can be provided to grow up to have a happy and healthy life.

We realize this wonderful opportunity would not be possible without you. We are more grateful than words could express.

Take care and thank you for making this possible.

Sincerely yours,
Elaine and David

They need three albums as the agency has three different locations. I mail the albums to Texas and wait to hear from the social worker who is taking care of us. I get a call in about a month's time. She tells me there is a birth mother who has interest in us, but after going through the album, realizes her baby will have an older sibling, so we are out.

The second call is about an 8-month-old little boy. We ask for a newborn, but consider the possibility. I contact our pediatrician and talk to old clients of mine in the mental health field and all of them have the same opinion. If the baby is less than twelve months old there is still time to bond.

We agree to adopt this baby boy. We make all the arrangements—plane tickets, hotel, rental car, cat sitter, etc. The phone rings the night before we are leaving. The agency tells us that the baby boy's biological maternal grandmother has decided to raise him. Very disappointing.

At this point we hire an adoption attorney in Texas to protect and help us. The attorney tells us that the next call with an available baby boy will require proof that the birth mother signs the appropriate papers before we plan another trip to Texas.

It is a week later when we get another call from Texas. The social worker says they have another 8-month-old baby boy. The birth mother picks us after seeing several albums. My 1-year-old baby picture and his are almost identical, and more than that, the Dear Birth Mommy letter impressed her.

We book the flight and we are on our way. We visit the foster parents' home, where the baby is, and then the adoption agency. Our attorney is with us.

What a delight, a healthy baby boy. We name him Peter Greg. Peter after my maternal grandfather, my Papa, the one who passed away when I was 2½, and for his middle name, Greg, in honor of Susan Greg. She is so ecstatic when we tell her.

Kate is so happy to have a baby brother. They are a little less than three years apart and Kate has such a nurturing soul, she often tells Peter what to do and watches over him. She is certainly a little mother in training. Peter also shares a birthday with my Dad.

When we bring Peter home we have a celebration at our home and our parents fly in. Henry and his new wife Sheri are there, along with friends and some of David's business associates. Jean and Miles promise to come. The day before the event, I get a call from Miles saying Jean isn't feeling well and they will not be able to come. This is surprising and disappointing. I have a feeling he isn't telling me the whole story.

Soon after, I find out that Jean is coughing up blood. She has lung cancer, and the rounds of chemotherapy start almost immediately. Several months go by and Miles is in constant touch; I hear from him almost every morning. I don't understand why, but illness is something that Miles finds difficult to handle, and the future is going to be difficult, draining and challenging all at the same time.

When Jean is feeling stronger after the chemo, we take a flight to the Midwest to see her. She is so stoic and strong and beautiful. It is an inspiration watching her handling the cancer and treatment. She is wearing a bandana on her head. She bends down and asks Kate and Peter if they want to touch her fuzzy head. She removes the bandana and they rub their little hands on her head. Jean looks up at me and smiles, as I choke back the tears.

Cancer is not kind to Jean; she is on a slippery slope downhill. When cancer spreads in the body, it usually moves up and that is what happens to Jean. The cancer moves from her lungs up to her brain. It is two long years that feels like an eternity. Then she passes away. Living so far from the Midwest, the daily conversations with Miles help keep me up to date and hopefully helps him get through each day. But for me I only imagine how awful the situation is and unfortunately, I am not able to be there at the end. So in a way I am fortunate to have my memories of Jean when she was well and whole. I still miss her every day. She is only 49 when she dies.

51

Kate is now four years old and we start to look for a house in a nearby town where the school district is one of the best. We find a subdivision being built, which we had seen before buying our current home. David and I both decided we didn't want to live there at the time, with construction going on and with all the noise and large trucks, etc. But now this same subdivision only has a few lots left to build on and it is in the school district we want for Kate and Peter. We sign an offer on the lot and put our house up for sale.

Where we are going to live reminds me of *Knots Landing* or *Desperate Housewives*. I think the idea of a subdivision makes me feel like I am back in the Midwest. I am wrong. David is traveling a lot on business, Kate is starting kindergarten and Peter will attend the same preschool as Kate. Game night, golf dates, dinner parties and more. I have no desire to keep up with it and feel like I am living in a fishbowl.

*

David and I are going to celebrate our tenth wedding anniversary in London. I welcome the time alone with him. We ask Kate's preschool teacher to stay with the kids, as she knows them well and has babysit on several occasions.

It is a glorious trip. We visit all the usual sites, Big Ben, Buckingham Palace and my favorite spot, Stratford on Avon. I had taken two years of Shakespeare in high school, and visiting Shakespeare's home and seeing *Richard III* at the Globe Theater is a dream come true. Back in London we enjoy seeing the British version of *Cats*, as well.

During our trip I talk with David about how I feel living in our new subdivision, and true to form, he says let's move. Always coming up with an instant solution, since David was the designer of our current home, and our builder agrees to let me hire the contractors, David says let's do it again. The real estate market is on the upswing, so why not? I enjoy the process, and we start looking for land to build another house—not an easy task in New England.

I receive a gift certificate to a local salon from a friend. It is on the other side of our town, which I don't frequent very often. On my way home, after my appointment, I think of a street/neighborhood to look at, near the salon. As I drive up the main road, I pass a street with the name Peter's Road. I do not remember seeing it before. I know the name of the street has to be a good sign. The next street I turn on is the one I am familiar with and there it is, a parcel of land, a sign, Lot for Sale by Owner. I stop the car and immediately call David at his office. He says, great, he will pull out the plans from our existing home, make some minor changes and we will build the house again. And so we do. I am the project manager again and spend 4 to 5 hours there a day. My builder stops by every day to be sure things are moving along well. And 11 months later we move into our new home.

*

Susan is on my mind and in my heart each and every day. She has to give up her apartment in the Midwest and move back to Alabama. Thankfully, her niece takes her in and cares for her in the last year of her life. Without Susan, I am not sure I would still be alive. She gave me so much strength, guidance to trust myself, unconditional love and support any time I needed it. We talk on the phone at least once a month. and Susan loves to write me letters. Thankfully, I have been saving them since 1989, and I have the last one she writes me in late 1996. Near the end I call Susan's niece once a week to see how Susan is doing and have her tell Susan how much I love her and to give her a big bear hug for me. Then I get the call Susan has passed away in her sleep late in December 2001. It is just like Susan; somehow, she doesn't want to go to heaven on the day I am born, and waits one more day to leave us. Susan is still here in spirit. I know that she was my guardian angel on earth and is my guardian angel from heaven.

A letter from Susan, exactly as she wrote it to me:

Hi Sweetie,

Just a note to say thank you
for the thought. And that Sweet
card. I was so glad to hear
From you. And to know that you are
Well. I Pray for your Every day that
God will For Ever Give you the Best.
I am Dong Very Well. It has been
So cold here. Until I just stay in the
House! Don't get out very much,
But today the Sun is Shining.
I Hope to go to Services to day.
I Hope when Ever you come
home that I Can See you. As it
Has been So Long. Well as Long as
You can Find Some one to Date. There
Is a Chance of Finding Some one.
But I Will Say this much about a
Date. Don't you be more concern about
Him to the point it Show. Let
Him Be More Concern about
You. I don't mean Don't you care for
Him. But let Him Care More For You.
(OK) Rember I Love You and Don't
Want to see (or) Hear of you Being
Hurt. Well I know you are tird of
Me by now (ok yes) My Christmas
Present was very nice. So you Give my love
To your parents. Again I say thank you for thinking about
me.

Love always,
Susan

52

It is time to find doctors in New England. Dr. Russ, my nephrologist from Johns Hopkins, refers me to Bryan Lee, MD, who is also a nephrologist. Dr. Russ says he knows Dr. Lee and he is very capable. I start to see Dr. Lee every four months for office visits and blood work. At the initial consult he doesn't like that I am taking lithium, and tells me that my kidney function potentially will continue to deteriorate because of it. This is not news to me, and once again I have to explain that if I go off the lithium, I risk having a manic episode and will end up in a psychiatric facility, or even worse, a state institution. I prefer quality of life even if it means having a shorter life. At least once a year Dr. Lee brings it up. He always whispers, which I find strange.

When we are reviewing my blood work together at one of my regular visits, I ask Dr. Lee why my calcium level is high. He says, "Oh that means you have a thyroid problem." I already know this as my endocrinologist has also been watching my calcium levels and told me so. I tell Dr. Lee I will schedule an appointment with Joan Disch, MD, my endocrinologist.

Dr. Disch says that the high calcium means that I now have parathyroid disease and she orders a thyroid nuclear medicine scan. The radiologist injects a radioactive substance into the vein in my arm, then uses a special camera to take an image of the thyroid. Even though normal procedure is for the doctor that orders the test to tell you the result, this time the radiologist runs into the room and says, "We see it! It is the right upper parathyroid gland that is the problem; it shows up on the monitor; it is normally very hard to see. I will call Dr. Disch immediately."

I have never heard of parathyroid glands. It is a fast learning curve. Dr. Disch explains that there are four parathyroid glands behind the thyroid gland, and that parathyroid glands control the amount of calcium in the blood and bones. She says the parathyroid gland that they see on the scan is an adenoma. An *adenoma* is a benign tumor that develops on top of the parathyroid gland. Dr. Disch tells me that this may be from the lithium toxicities. She immediately refers me to a thyroid surgeon to have the adenoma surgery. Once again the lithium toxicities are affecting another part of my body. I obviously have no control and don't know what will come next. I am scared.

*

We sell our house and are living in a carriage house while we build our new house. Kate is five and Peter is almost three. David is traveling for business a couple days a week, which is an improvement from Monday through Friday.

Richard Green, MD, is the surgeon who will remove the adenoma. Prior to surgery, he has me sign consent papers, which state if I lose my voice after the surgery, he is not liable. He laughs and tells me in his twenty years of performing this type of surgery that has only happened once. Dr. Green tells me that he is going to schedule the surgery as soon as possible, because of the size of the adenoma. He says he will remove the adenoma and snip a piece off of one of the three remaining parathyroid glands to send to pathology.

David and I get to the hospital at 5:30 a.m., and the nurses start to prep me for the surgery. The anesthesiologist comes in and tells me he is going to insert medication in my line to help me relax. I share with him that I do not require the normal dose, in fact much less because of my renal issues. He assures me that he will cut the dose in half. As the team of doctors and nurses wheel me into the operating room, I look up at the enormous lights and tell them they look like wildflowers. They all laugh and say the medication is working well.

The next thing I know I am back in my hospital room. Dr. Green is there and asks me how I am feeling. I open my mouth, but the words don't come out. He gives me a drink of water and says to try again. I am unable to talk. Dr. Green starts yelling at me and David, "How can this be happening now?" I am ruining his record, two in twenty years that can't talk after he performs the parathyroid surgery. And he storms out of the room. David and I shake our heads in disbelief, finding his behavior surprisingly unprofessional. Several hours pass and Dr. Green comes back to see me. There is no apology, just letting me know that if my voice does not come back by the end of the year, he will have to do another surgery. That sure isn't going to happen if I have anything to do with it.

A couple of days later David takes me home from the hospital. He buys me a whistle to get the kids' attention when they are playing outdoors, and I flicker the lights to get their attention inside. It is such an odd feeling, I automatically try to talk and nothing comes out. And when the phone rings, I somehow try to communicate, which is futile and the callers hang up on me. To help my throat heal, I drink what seems like gallons of hot tea and I use up several squeezable honey bears.

I see Dr. Green for a postoperative visit and he seems to be calmer. He says that the reason I have lost my voice is because he had to unwind one of my vocal cords, which had been wrapped around the adenoma. He wants to see me once a month to see if there is gradual progress. Finally, when I visit him in January, my voice is back, but not completely. Meaning, if I raise my voice it hurts my throat, and yelling is out of the question. He says further surgery is not going to be necessary. Always trying to find the good in life experiences, I make jokes with my family and friends that I am a kinder, gentler person, because I can no longer raise my voice or yell.

53

It is May and we move into our new home; very exciting times. It takes about a month to unpack. Minutes after I am done David comes home from the office on a Wednesday afternoon. He tells me he has to be in Paris for a conference the following Monday. Will I be able to join him? It is 2001. I have to call American Express to transfer points for flights. They tell me there is a 48-hour turnaround and I explain that my timeline is short. They work with me and email me the ticket in 24 hours. I call my friend Mary, who always has a few babysitters up her sleeve, and presto, kids will have care, and Monday morning I am flying to Paris with David!

We are there for five days and I meet a woman from Minnesota who is there with her husband for the same conference as David. She and I tour together and she informs me that the Louvre Museum is open Wednesday evening until 9 p.m. David gets back to the hotel at 5:30 p.m. on Wednesday and we take the equivalent of our American subway to the Louvre. We literally run through the halls of the Museum to get to the Mona Lisa. When we get there, we see how small the painting actually is. The canvas is only 31 by 21 inches and there are people everywhere. The Louvre is enormous, and we don't have much time to linger, so we walk as quickly as we can to try to take it all in. We are holding hands as we walk. It works out well for me, so that I can look at the ceilings, which are so beautiful to behold.

54

We have been home from Paris for a couple of months and David's birthday is approaching. We talk about renewing our wedding vows, as it will be our 12th year wedding anniversary. I suggest that it be our birthday gift to each other, since my birthday is in December and David's is January. We choose his birthday for the day. It is just the four of us, David, Kate, Peter and me. Here are our wedding vows to each other:

David,

Since the day I met you, my life has changed for the better. You have stood beside me in some very painful and frightening times. I am glad to say you never left my side and these times have made us stronger.

You have shown me how wonderful it can be to have you love me so much that when we are together at home, you follow me from room to room, "because you enjoy my company."

I look forward to spending every possible moment together with you for the rest of our lives, enjoying being close to each other and having open communication and always feeling connected. I know we both enjoy our projects and adventures and all the pleasure and conversations that go along with them.

But most of all, I am thrilled to say that my love for you continues to grow on a daily basis. You are a terrific husband and father and all around provider, along with being the best problem solver and handyman I know. You are sensitive, determined, caring, funny, special, romantic and generous and my best friend. The list is infinite!

The best part of all is you are MINE!

I Love You Forever,
Elaine

*

Elaine,

This is a very exciting day for me. Not many people feel the same way we do after so many years. And I hope you know that what this says is in my heart and how excited I am about marrying you all over again. I think we are stronger, closer and having more fun than we ever have.

I want you to know that I love you and I always have, from the first day that we met. I think we make a good team; when we work together on things, they always turn out better than expected.

I want you to know that I think you are the best when it comes to raising the kids. As you know we have the best behaved kids that we know and we are recognized as having such, by the comments that people continually make.

I don't always say it, but I know that you take great care of me, all the time. I don't know anyone who has it as good as I do. I just want to say thank you. Elaine, I love you! This is the very best birthday gift I could ever have.

I love you forever,
David

*

One morning my arms are full of clothes for the cleaners as I am coming down the back stairway and I miss a step and fall. I hear my ankle make a loud cracking sound. David happens to be standing in the mudroom putting his coat on for work and asks me if I am OK. I say, "Oh no that sounds bad, there goes my ankle, I am going to be fat." I have been walking five miles a day for months and I will not be doing that now. After a visit to the emergency room, I come home with a splint on my ankle and crutches. I do not have a broken ankle, but it is a bad sprain and I need to wear the splint for one month, which is twice as long as normal.

I have a regular appointment with Dr. Lee to check my kidney function the next day and I tell him my plan to lose twenty-five pounds. I ask him if a weight loss like this can help my kidney function. He says it certainly can help. He once again mentions the lithium and how it will be best to discontinue taking it, to retain my kidney function. I ask him why he lowers his voice when he says this. It always makes me feel bad, like he doesn't want to say it too loud, so no one knows I am manic depressive. Really no different than my parents or some other doctors I have come across who judge me. It is disappointing.

I am ready to do everything I can to lose the weight. I am five foot, seven inches and one hundred fifty pounds, medium-size bones and wear a size ten. I carry my weight well, but that isn't the point. I am already eating healthy food, I just need to decrease my portion size and drink more water. I want to lose the weight to hopefully improve my kidney function.

In six weeks, I lose fifteen pounds and David is unhappy about me becoming too thin. I laugh and tell him that will never happen; I like food too much. It takes me two more months to take off the last ten pounds, and I am going to keep it off. I am eating healthfully before I lose the weight; it is my portion size that needed to be cut, a lifestyle change, not a diet.

I know it is time to make a change, to look for another nephrologist to get another opinion. I call my friend Maggie in Florida who has recently married a man who specializes in placing nephrologists into medical practices. She hands the phone to Larry. He doesn't know most of my medical history, but I share enough with him for him to be able to suggest the right kind of specialist. I tell him I need a doctor who will answer the hard questions. He suggests Lawrence Ming, MD. Larry knows that he is one of the three top specialists in the country who sees patients who have renal issues from lithium.

My luck is holding. Dr. Ming has a cancellation later this week. His receptionist says that it usually takes three months to get an appointment for a consultation. I have my list of questions ready for Dr. Ming. I am already sitting in his office when he walks in. He is short in statue, but I can feel his presence in a powerful way. He is intimidating even before he speaks. He listens and types my medical history at the same time. I tell him that I need to know what the lithium is going to do to my remaining kidney function. I tell him Dr. Lee skirts around answering my hard questions. The two most important questions: will I need to be on dialysis at some point and will I need a kidney transplant?

Dr. Ming looks up from his monitor and clearly says that if I do not go off the lithium, I will need dialysis in ten years. I am 45 years old. I am not in shock from what he says, just numb. I visit the place inside me where I start watching him as if it isn't me and someone else is sitting there; a means to protect myself. Intimidating or not, I have to put all my trust in Dr. Ming at this point to save the remainder of my kidney function. He tells me it isn't his specialty to make the change in medication, and obviously if I am on lithium, I will need to see a psychiatrist to change the meds. He refers me to the manic-depressive clinic to see a psychiatrist there, Dr. Mark Stone, and he asks me if I am seeing a psychologist, as that will be helpful to form a triangle of care including him while changing medication.

I do have a psychologist, but he is moving from the suburbs to the city, which means at least a two-hour round trip to see him. We try phone sessions, which really don't work, so I ask him if he can speak to the head of the practice, James Irving, PhD, to see if he is taking new patients. He does that and I am happy to hear that Dr. Irving is taking new patients and he is willing to see me. I make an appointment to see him and also to have a consultation with Mark Stone, MD, at the manic-depressive clinic. Usually one will have a psychiatrist onboard to prescribe the lithium; however, my internist is willing to do this for me, as long as I get periodic blood tests to make sure the lithium level is therapeutic, within normal range.

David comes along for my consult with Dr. Stone. Once again, I have to repeat my medical history and find that safe place inside and listen to what I am saying as if it is someone else is speaking.

David is there for support and does not add anything to the conversation at this point.

Dr. Stone asks how many times I have cycled since I was a teenager and diagnosed with bipolar disorder. *Bipolar disorder*, that term makes me fume. The term for *manic depression* was officially changed to *bipolar* in 1968, five years before I was even diagnosed, but it wasn't even used by psychiatrists until much later. It seems like fluff to me. Why change the name to make it sound prettier, when underneath, it is the same thing? My understanding of *cycling* is that even if I take lithium for my manic-depressive illness, every twelve to eighteen months it may not work. If that happens, the medication is useless, and one has a breakthrough episode of mania or depression.

However, in my case, I never, ever cycled. Dr. Stone found this very interesting and says possibly I am not manic-depressive after all, but that he isn't going to be the one responsible for taking me off of lithium. Once labeled/diagnosed with such a severe mental disorder, or more accurately a chemical imbalance, he isn't willing to take responsibility—but that is a choice *I* can make.

We are in a daze. Dr. Stone suggests that instead, I pick one of eight other pharmaceuticals currently on the market for bipolar disorder. He writes down the names of the medications and hands me the piece of paper. He says at this point it is obvious to him that both David and I are very intelligent and will be able to explore each and every one of the eight medications. He tells us to give him a call in a week or two after we have time to research them. Dr. Stone does say that Abilify is the drug of choice in his opinion. No wonder there are Abilify mugs, notepads and pens all over his desk. It seems clear to us that the pharmaceutical company owns him.

We both research the eight medications. David is far more analytical than I am and digs deeper than I can. But what is obvious to both of us rather quickly is that all eight meds have side effects that can compromise another organ of mine. We agree that I cannot afford to do this.

During this time, I also begin to see James Irving, my new psychologist. I click with him immediately. That is very fortunate, because oftentimes when people seek a professional for therapy, one may have to try out a few until they find a good fit. Again, my luck is holding. Given that, I have close to an hour session with James once a week, he is familiar with my medical history and is in the loop. He speaks with Dr. Ming and tells me he has no interest in speaking to Dr. Stone.

What comes next is life-altering. James insists I am not manic-depressive. He says I have been misdiagnosed—and he is very firm about it. I tell him that can't be possible, and if he is suggesting I go off the lithium and not pick one of the eight medications that Dr. Stone tells me to choose from, that I will lose my quality of life and end up in a psychiatric facility or state institution for life. I tell James this is unacceptable and that I will take quality of life any day of the week even if that means dying younger because of ultimate kidney failure. And who knows if I will find a kidney donor?

This dialogue goes on with James for a couple of weeks. He insists I see a different psychiatrist away from the large hospitals in the downtown area, where even he agrees psychiatrists are under the control of pharmaceutical giants. James refers me to a psychiatrist he knows, who practices in the suburbs, Theodore Watson, MD.

I book a consult, and he spends two hours with me. Dr. Watson is from England, and he is extremely patient and puts me at ease. Not an easy thing to do. At the end of the consult, he says unequivocally that I am not manic-depressive, and that I need to titrate off the lithium immediately.

It is finally becoming clear that James and Dr. Watson, and even the pompous idiot Dr. Stone, are all in agreement. It is true. I have been taking lithium for thirty years and have never needed it! I was brained-washed all these years...and now have permanent organ damage—and that has left me with chronic illnesses, to say the least.

We never know what the future holds, but now I am madder than ever at the poor, foolish decisions that were made about my health by my mother! She is the sick one with a mental illness.

James and Dr. Watson help wean me off the lithium. They suggest I do this over six weeks' time, and I make up a schedule for twelve weeks and show it to them. I want to go off as slowly as possible, not knowing how I will feel.

As soon as I no longer have a therapeutic level of lithium onboard, meaning the medication is not doing anything once it is below the therapeutic level, I begin feeling like I am speeding. I experience a tight feeling in my chest and my blood pressure goes up. James keeps reminding me that I have been under sedation for thirty years and my body has to find a new normal, not having the lithium onboard. There is no question about that. I actually look for an exit hatch, a way to unzip myself and walk away from my body. James insists that I have to be patient and that there will be an adjustment period. (It takes over two years!) Dr. Ming raises the dosage of my blood pressure medication, which helps to some degree.

55

We are both 47 and David has an opportunity to speak at a conference in Rimini, Italy. He insists that I go with him, to relax and get away from everything and all the doctors. How fortunate I am to have such a caring partner in life. I immediately start to plan care for the kids, etc., and before I know it we are on our way. We fly to Milan and take a train through the countryside, with stops in Lodi, Parma, Modena, Forti, Cesena, and finally arriving in Rimini. The trip is just what I need. There are quiet dinners in the evening and I spend lazy days touring, shopping and eating the most delicious food.

We return home feeling well rested and ready for the next adventure. Unfortunately, not all adventures have a happy ending. David's Mom isn't doing well. She is in the hospital and needs surgery for a tumor in her shoulder. The cancer has spread to her lungs and there isn't much time left. She is such a vital woman, always helping others and loves her family. She passes away in September 2004, at 82. I am frustrated, wishing she would have sought medical care sooner and possibly gotten the tumor removed before it spread to her lungs and killed her.

Two weeks later my father is in the hospital. He has had the battery in his pacemaker changed and his heart valve has become infected. He is 82, going on 102. My mother never listens to my advice about anything, but surprisingly this time she does listen to advice I give her, and it helps keep him alive the last few years of his life. He is now at a Heart Institute waiting for heart surgery.

He doesn't make it, and he dies on September 28th. A hurricane comes through Florida the night before his death and a second hurricane comes through two days later, making it almost impossible to get his body back to the Midwest in time for the funeral service.

Again, as luck has it, David and I and the kids had a visit to see Dad in August, six weeks before he passed away. We usually travel to Florida in April and December during school breaks. We made a special trip for my friend Maggie's family party and we were able to visit with my Mom and Dad. Dad was using a walker by then, and was having dialysis three times a week. He never complained and always had a smile on his face.

This is Dad's eulogy September 30, 2004.

Kind of Person Dad Was

My Dad was the kind of person who was upbeat and kind. He was always thankful for every day. And he had a beautiful smile, loved to give tight hugs and would always reach out his hand for me to hold. He especially loved babies. He would see a newborn baby and say, "There is a fresh one." His favorite fruit was bananas. Dad would say that was because they had no bones in them. But most of all when it came to Dad's health, he was a fighter. He seemed to have nine lives, coming back from illnesses that the doctors said were the end. Thankfully, many times the doctors were wrong.

Meaningful Memories I Have of Dad

My dad was a special person. I remember when I was a little girl and how he carried me to the bakery to get a cookie. He had a huge grin on his face as he introduced me to everyone. It made me feel like a princess! Another wonderful memory was of a summer over thirty years ago. The whole family was helping to stock the new hardware store he had bought. At the end of the summer, Dad gave me a Brother sewing machine, which I still use today.

Lessons Learned

Lesson 1— As you know, Dad had a teaching degree; he graduated from university at twenty. Dad was my teacher and tutor. I remember many English lessons with him. Dad always stressed the importance of continuing education.

Lesson 2— When dealing with people, Dad would say "Kill them with kindness." By following this advice I have avoided many headaches. He was right.

Inspirations

In Dad's golden years I found many times that he inspired me. One time about fifteen years ago, I asked him, "As you are getting older do you get depressed?" And his answer was clear, "No not at all. I am thankful for every day I have to enjoy life."

Memories

Dad was truly a loving man. I know that my father loved me with his whole heart and adored our children. He never stopped telling us that. But most of all he adored my mother for over sixty-one years. A gift was given to us, with our last visit to Mom and Dad in August. Dad looked wonderful and he was vibrant and thrilled to see us as we were thrilled to see him.

Dad, I will miss you always.

Dad, I will love you always.

Dad, I will remember you always.

Your baby girl

56

A couple of months later I receive a call from the hospital after having my yearly mammogram. The radiologist wants to repeat the test. The repeat mammogram is done on my right breast only. The doctor comes in and says there is calcification that is starting to form in a circular shape and that I can come back in six months for a recheck. I thank him and tell him I want a copy of the films now please.

I call my gynecologist, David Daily, MD, and he says if I am more comfortable seeing a breast surgeon now, instead of waiting six months for another mammogram, he is suggesting a local center, which is in the neighborhood. I once again thank him and tell him I will look for a breast surgeon downtown. It has just hit me that I never thought this would happen to me. I am in a daze.

I do my research and call a hospital downtown, which is well known for their breast department. The clerk tells me that I can drop off my films and the radiologist will call me when they have a chance to review the films, but at this time they are behind and she isn't sure when they can get back to me. Not wanting to wait, I ask the receptionist for a recommendation and she mentions Susan Ryan, MD. She said Dr. Ryan had her training there and is now head of the department at another downtown hospital. Before I make the call, I call my friend Amanda, who has two friends who are going through breast cancer. Both happen to be seeing Dr. Ryan. It quickly becomes clear and I make an appointment with Dr. Ryan.

Dr. Ryan examines the mammogram films and tells me she wants to do an outpatient surgery to take a biopsy of the calcification. The morning of the surgery, David is with me and reminds me to ask the anesthesiologist to put something in my IV to stop the nausea that I can get from anesthesia. The doctor is happy to do it and I wake up in recovery feeling like it is easier than a root canal, except for the part where the radiologist sticks a long wire into my breast while viewing my breast with an ultrasound machine. The wire needs to stay there during the surgery as a marker for the surgeon. I am grateful that the anesthesiologist has also given me a little something to help with the pain.

Then we wait, one week for the biopsy results. Dr. Ryan calls a few moments before the school bus drops Kate off. She tells me I have DCIS, which is ductal carcinoma in situ, and that I will need another surgery to get a clean margin, then radiation. I feel like I can't breathe. I have no idea what she is talking about. What does it all mean? I have so many questions, but Kate is going to be at the front door any minute and I don't want her to hear me talking to the surgeon, until I understand what she is saying. I ask Dr. Ryan if I can call her back when David gets home from work and we can both talk to her.

David and I get a quick lesson from Dr. Ryan about DCIS and radiation. She tells us that DCIS is the most common type of noninvasive breast cancer. *Ductal* because the cancer starts in the milk ducts, and *in situ* means in its original place. She says that DCIS isn't life-threatening, but having it can increase the risk of developing an invasive breast cancer later on. She says that most recurrences happen within five to ten years after the initial diagnosis and the chances of it recurring are around 30%. By having radiation, I could cut that percentage in half.

I schedule the second surgery for the clean margins and make an appointment with the radiation oncologist. Dr. Ryan suggests I use a clinic closer to home that is an affiliate of the hospital, being that I will go for radiation treatments five days a week for six weeks. I have a consultation with Jessica Kong, MD, who after setting up my radiation treatment orders a consult with an oncologist and genetic counselor.

The fact is I know very little about breast cancer and my head is spinning from all these appointments. The genetic counselor tells me that there are two different blood tests to find out if I have the mutated gene. We all have the gene that can cause cancer, but they want to determine if it is mutated or not. They will draw the blood today in two tubes and send them off for testing. She also asks me my family history. My maternal grandfather, my Papa, had breast cancer and a mastectomy in the early 1950s. My mother had breast cancer at 80, associated with taking estrogen replacement for thirty-five years. The genetic counselor tells me they don't count my mother as having breast cancer for a genetic reason, being that it came from the estrogen replacement. And even though her father, my Papa, had breast cancer, genetic testing was not available then.

I stand to leave, and she asks me if I want to know what they suggest if I have the mutation. I turn around and look at her as I am holding the doorknob. She tells me that if I have the mutated gene, she will recommend I have bilateral mastectomies and have my ovaries removed. I turn the knob and somehow get to my car and call David from my cell. I tell him what the genetic counselor says, and he says that can't be true. It takes me fifteen minutes to get home. By the time I reach the door, David has already done research on what the genetic counselor told me. He is white as a ghost. Everything the counselor says is true.

I am numb, but that never stops me from moving forward. I call Tina, a friend of mine who is a radiologist, and tell her about my visit to the genetic counselor. I ask her if I can wait to have radiation until after the test results come back; why do I want to have radiation to my breast if it is going to be removed? She says to wait for the blood test results, since it is DCIS and not urgent to complete the radiation right away. I call Dr. Kong and ask her to stop the treatments for now. I have only received two treatments. Dr. Kong says it will be fine if I wait. All that keeps going through my mind is that having the radiation while waiting for the genetic blood work is a money-making proposition for the hospital, just like any other business.

My next appointment is a consultation with an oncologist, Harry Franklin, MD. David is with me. I tell Dr. Franklin that I am experiencing a great deal of pain in my breast after the first two treatments. He says this is odd, that most women have no pain from radiation treatments. He suggests that I speak to my breast surgeon about having a mastectomy and leaving the lymph nodes. That way I will not have any more pain if I decide to continue the radiation treatments after the genetic testing comes back. David and I look at each other and then glare at Dr. Franklin and leave.

I call Dr. Ryan, my breast surgeon, when we get home. and she says something that is very uncharacteristic for a surgeon to say. She completely disagrees with what Dr. Franklin suggests. Why would I want to do that Dr. Ryan asks. That is very aggressive. She recommends that for now I wait for the genetic test results to return and she will help me find another oncologist.

So we wait. It has been three weeks and three days. I call the genetic counselor, who had told me it would be three weeks at most before we got the results. She tells me that she will call the lab in Utah. Hard to believe there is only one lab in the whole United States that does this testing. Talk about a monopoly. She calls me back and tells me that both the BRAC1 and BRAC2 tests are negative and now I can contact the radiation oncologist to restart the radiation treatments.

I start the radiation treatments again, twenty-eight more. Each day while sitting in the waiting room in a hospital gown, waiting to go in for my treatment, the same women are waiting too. As our appointments are at the same time each day, I meet many courageous women, who have been diagnosed with much more serious breast cancer than mine. The one thing I hear on several occasions from three or more women is, "I am back for my other breast. I had breast cancer on the other side five years ago." That information stays with me.

I get a call from Dr. Ryan. She asks me if I have interest in being in a breast ultrasound study that is starting in December. It is a three-year study. I respond yes, that I am very happy to be part of the study to help other women.

The intake coordinator Kathy calls me soon after to take a medical history over the phone and then I meet with her to sign the study documents. I will be having a mammogram and come back one week later for the ultrasound, and I will get the results of both tests two weeks from the date of the mammogram. The regular procedure is to get all the results immediately after the test; however, with a study, all the doctors that are part of the study have to review it before the patient can get the results.

We wait. Two weeks go by and I call Kathy. She asks me to hold on while she checks. She says that the results are in and that something is wrong. It is my left breast, which is my breast that we think does not have cancer. I find this shocking. Why would Kathy, the study coordinator, be telling me this? Why hasn't the radiologist given me a call yet? I tell Kathy I want to speak with the radiologist immediately. She says she will have her call me within the hour. I like the radiologist. She is from the Midwest area too and we reminisced during the ultrasound.

The phone rings thirty minutes later. The radiologist tells me that I have a stage 1 tumor in my left breast. Again, I find this shocking. How can she be telling me this without a biopsy? The biopsy is going to be at 8 a.m. the next day. I am a wreck. I call a few friends to make arrangements for the kids to get to school the next day. David and I don't sleep a wink.

I have to lie flat on my back on a cold hard table. The radiologist is there along with a nurse and the surgeon. The surgeon makes two attempts that do not reach the tumor. Even though they numb the area, it is painful. Finally, on the third attempt, the surgeon reaches the tumor, pulls back on the syringe and a tan creamy substance fills the syringe. She says, "I am glad to tell you it is a cyst, not a tumor. This was a false positive." David and I are both in shock, but it is a good kind of shock. I know that it is against protocol for the radiologist to tell me it is stage 1 cancer before a biopsy, but I don't want to put any energy into reporting her. I move on.

57

I try to take some time to reflect. Life is moving so quickly that I do not often have time to do this. I remind myself that the thyroid and breast cancers and surgeries are just bleeps on my radar. For now, I just need time to recover and I will bounce back quickly.

The real challenges are living with chronic illness and post-traumatic stress disorder; the first being the hardest. I have labile hypertension from the renal insufficiency, caused by the lithium toxicity. It is not your garden-style hypertension; it is more like a roller coaster. Stress, whether it is good or bad, internal or external, triggers it.

They say high blood pressure is a silent killer. I truly believe this, because when it was first detected in Annapolis, I had no idea it was high. Over time I have learned to listen to my body, and when I have a headache, it can mean one of two things, either my blood pressure is high or low. When it is high, I need to take additional blood pressure medication, and when it is low, the only thing I can do to raise it is to eat salty food. I make it sound simple, but it isn't.

Some days it is really hard not to hate my mother for letting all this happen to me. Her pushing the psychiatrist to raise the dosage of the lithium, her blatant absence of understanding or caring about the consequences of her actions—all resulting in misdiagnoses, years of taking medications I should not have been, resulting in massive organ damage, and a lifetime of illness!

The post-traumatic stress disorder was caused by the hallucinations from the toxicity, when we were in that hotel room in Indiana and I thought my parents had hired an assassin to kill me. Whenever I walk into a hotel room, it doesn't cross my mind, unless the room is set up the same way as the one that horrific night in Indiana. When I am with David and the kids, I remind myself that I am safe and try to ignore it.

A few years ago, I was away on business and had to spend one night alone in a hotel. I walked into the room and it was exactly like the one in Indiana, but I was exhausted and thought I could handle it, knowing far well, all I had to do is go back to the reception desk and ask for another room. I didn't sleep the whole night. I kept calling David at home and he would talk with me, and I kept the TV and every light on and had the shower curtain in the bathroom pulled as far open as possible. My eyes didn't leave the doorknob from the connecting door to make sure it wasn't moving. I flew home in the morning and slept the whole way. I promised myself I would not make that same mistake again.

58

It is 2006. Life keeps going and we have a late spring as always in New England, and a perfect summer. We spend many days at the beach and really enjoy ourselves. July 4th, there are the annual fireworks at the beach. My stomach is bothering me, so I tell David and the kids to go to the fireworks without me, which is unlike me. We always do things together as a family, but I don't want them to miss the fun. I sleep for a while when they are gone and wake up with more severe pain on the right side. I think it might be appendicitis, since David had an emergency appendectomy two years before and my symptoms are similar to his. I call my internist, which I know is futile, because he will tell me that I have to go to the ER, which is exactly what he says.

David and the kids arrive home soon after and take me to the local hospital. The ER doc orders a CAT scan with contrast. I tell him I will have to check with my nephrologist because I don't think I can have contrast, as it can be damaging to my remaining kidney function. They get Dr. Ming's office on the line, but he is out of town and Dr. Miles is covering. He speaks with me and tells me to not allow them to use the contrast, and he prefers that I get to the hospital downtown. Unfortunately, the highway is not open on 4th of July, being so close to the river where they are launching fireworks. So, I stay put.

The CAT scan is done without contrast and they admit me to the hospital. David takes the kids home for the night. In the morning the surgeon comes into the room. I recognize him, because he had done David's appendectomy. He tells me that they do not know what is wrong. The x-ray shows nothing on the right side of my abdomen. He cannot explain the pain I am having and says he will come back later to see me.

The surgeon returns in an hour and says he has news for me. He sits down and tells me the good news—they found out why I am having pain. The hospital's radiologist read the film and found a large tumor on my left kidney, and the pain I am having must be referred pain, which he says is somewhat common when diagnosing abdominal issues.

I tell him I do not understand and need more explanation. Why doesn't he have this information the first time he comes in the room? He explains that the film had been sent out overnight to India for a radiologist to read there and that the order had read "rule out appendicitis," which translates to: the radiologist only looked at the right side of the film. If the radiologist at the local hospital had not looked at the whole film, the tumor would have gone undetected — and might not have been detected until it was too late. I call my sister-in-law Sheri's good friend Betty, who is a urologist in New York City. The surgeon at the hospital tells me that a urologist is the kind of surgeon who does this type of surgery.

Betty has me read the whole report to her and she stops me when I get to the part that says it is 6 centimeters and encapsulated. She tells me that if it is 7 centimeters it can burst and spread the cancer though out my abdomen to all my organs. Silence, I have nothing to say. I can hardly breathe. Betty says these types of tumors are often malignant and the fact that it is encapsulated is excellent news. Once I can speak again, I say, "But Betty, cancer moves up." She repeats that it is encapsulated, but suggests that before the surgeon discharges me from the hospital, I need to ask him to order a CAT scan of my chest to see if the cancer is there, for my piece of mind. The CAT scan is negative, nothing abnormal in the chest. I go home that evening.

That night, David and I spend a couple of hours doing research about large kidney tumors. We are each using our own computer to gather the information faster. We then get in bed together to review what we find. I tell David that it looks like there are two ways to do the surgery. Option one is a laparoscopy, the least invasive way, where the surgeon makes an incision near the belly button and then pulls the tumor out. The second way is a partial nephrectomy, where a six- to seven-inch incision is made in the abdomen to get directly to the kidney. While still attached, the kidney is pulled out of the abdomen, the tumor is cut off the kidney, and the kidney is then put back. The second looks like my only option, because I don't want the doctor to pull the tumor over my other organs, in case it bursts.

The next morning I call my cousin George, who is an internist and the CEO of a hospital on the west coast. His help is invaluable. I fill him in on all the details and he tells me he will get back to me within the hour as to which urologist in the New England area is the right one. Dr. Ming is still out of town, so I cannot rely on him for advice or a referral. I can call his partner, but do not know him or have any level of trust in him. George calls back and tells me of a group of urologists he recommends. It is surprising that he doesn't pick a hospital downtown. We discuss it and he tells me that the urology department he picks is one of the best in the country. He says he will call there immediately and speak with the urologist he knows and let him know I will be calling. I can't thank him enough and I call David at his office to share the news. The call waiting beeps through and I see it says Urology Associates. I tell David I will call him right back.

59

John Bruno, MD, is the senior partner in the group of urologists George recommended, and the one who has the most experience with partial nephrectomies. Because of George's call I am seen within two days. Before my consultation with Dr. Bruno, he orders a three-dimensional MRI. When I schedule the appointment, they ask me if I am claustrophobic and suggest I take something to relax an hour prior to the MRI to help me through it. I wish it was that easy. This is the first MRI for me and I remember having a client in Florida who was a radiologist. My office was near the MRI room and I could hear patients crying most of the day.

First, they hand me earplugs to put in my ears, then I lie down on a hard tube-like table that is concave. The technician puts a hard plastic board over my chest and abdomen and places my arms at my sides. It gets worse from there. Next, large Velcro straps crisscross over my body holding my arms and the plastic board in place. The technician covers me with a blanket and puts a panic button in my right hand and tells me that once they put me into the MRI machine, I can just push the button if I can't handle it. But I realize that will just prolong the agony, because once he takes me out of the tube and talks to me for a minute or two, he will put me right back into the MRI tunnel in order to complete the test. My body starts going into the tube and I will have to close my eyes. If I don't I will see the inside of the tube and start to panic.

The test takes about thirty minutes and the tech talks to me from the next room, which has a large glass window so he can see me, and protects him from radiation. He tells me when to hold my breath and when I can breathe. The machine has very loud sounds that keep repeating that remind me of gunshots I've heard in movies. They keep going off and I start to sob, very quietly, but don't dare to move, afraid they might have to keep me in the tube longer if I am not still.

The next morning, I meet Dr. Bruno. He comes into the exam room and greets me with a beautiful smile. I get a sense right away that he is very charming and has nice bedside manner.

I don't wait for him to start the conversation. I know that my cousin told Dr. Bruno my situation and I say to him, "As you know I only have half my kidney function left and I have three older brothers who all owe me, so tell me now if after the surgery I am going to wake up and be on dialysis and need a kidney transplant. I hope that one of my brothers is a match. He roars with laughter and gives me a hug and tells me to come with him. He takes me to the x-ray box outside the exam room and turns on the light to show me the 3-D MRI results. The 6-centimeter tumor is at the bottom of my left kidney. He says he will do a partial nephrectomy and literally take my kidney out of my body, cut off the tumor and put my kidney back. And he says that I should not lose any of my remaining kidney function. He explains that the reason I may have the tumor is the large amount of iodine that was given to me originally by the endocrinologists who were trying to diagnose me when I was a teenager.

Dr. Bruno then walks me over to the surgical scheduling desk and tells them to give me his next opening for the surgery. We shake hands and he says he has never had an experience with a patient like me; usually it is his job to make the patient laugh. The surgery is on a Friday in August 2006. It will be a three-hour surgery.

We discuss the fact that I might need a pint of blood after the surgery, so I stop at the blood bank to make an appointment to donate a pint of my blood. The phlebotomist draws a CBC (complete blood count) and then a nurse speaks with me.

She asks me if I know that my hematocrit is low, and I tell her I know I am anemic due to my renal insufficiency. She is curt and very short with me, very rude and unprofessional, and tells me that I can't donate blood with that low of a hematocrit, and she doesn't understand how I can walk around all day and feel good with such a low count. I say thanks so much and leave. Thinking, thanks for nothing. David offers to donate a pint of blood for me; fortunately, we are the same blood type. It is one less thing to worry about, and somehow he always knows what to do to put me at ease.

Dr. Bruno comes in to see me right before the surgery. I already have the IV in my arm and have met the anesthesiologist and the two surgical nurses. He takes my hand and tells me everything is going to be fine, he is sure of it. I thank him and close my eyes and pray he is right. I wake up in recovery and David is already there at my side, along with the anesthesiologist. I am in recovery for three hours, which is much longer than normal, because I have many tubes going into and out of my body and they want to make sure everything is flowing properly before they move me to my hospital room.

They finally take me to my room, position me on the bed on my back and wrap something around my legs. They are like inflatable boots without the foot part, to help the circulation in my legs, to avoid blood clots. They put a catheter in my bladder, and insert a chest tube, a tube right below the incision for drainage, and let's not forget the IV in my arm for fluids and medications.

It is Peter's birthday two days after my surgery and I really want the kids to come and visit, but do not take into account how bad I must look. David doesn't have the heart to tell me or keep the kids from visiting. They stay for about an hour and I explain what all the tubes are for. They gently kiss me good-bye and David takes them home.

While he is gone I sleep awhile, and when I wake up I notice that my arm that has the IV in it is swollen, twice as large as my other arm. I push the call button for the nurse. She comes in and I show her my arm. She totally dismisses it. I push the button again after she leaves and another nurse comes in and says, "OH MY, it looks like your IV infiltration." All the fluid is going into my arm not my vein. She calls the anesthesiologist. There is a group of doctors rotating care for patients, and a doctor comes in and restarts the IV in my other arm and checks on me two more times that day.

So, now it is already Sunday afternoon and I have been asking since early Saturday morning when Dr. Bruno will be in to see me. David asks as well and the standard answer is, "He will be in later today." An intern who is taking care of me visits and has a bad attitude every time I ask him about Dr. Bruno. Finally, Tuesday morning, Dr. Bruno walks in, all smiles, how am I doing? I am ready to scream. I ask where he has been and isn't it customary for the surgeon to come in the day after surgery to see how his patients are doing? He says yes, but it was his son's birthday and he left right after my surgery and thought it would be better not to tell me. Both Dr. Bruno and I had wanted to get the surgery done asap to avoid the risk of the tumor bursting inside of me, so I understand why he did it when he did, but he could have told me he was going out of town. At this point I just want to go home. All the tubes are taken out and David takes me home.

*

I spend the next two weeks resting and recovering. My friend and neighbor Jenna makes arrangements for meals for our family for a month. She talks me into it and I'm glad she does. I have a postop visit with Dr. Bruno, and he orders future MRIs, CAT scans and blood work. The pathology shows that the tumor is totally malignant as Betty predicts, but the surgery is a success. The fact that the tumor was still encapsulated saves my life. I am very fortunate. Once I recover and am back on my feet, I remind myself that when you need surgery, there is only one thing that matters, you find the best surgeon for the job. The rest of it doesn't matter.

60

Before I know it, it is December, and it is the second year of my obligation to the breast ultrasound study. Believe me, I have doubts after last year's false positive, but know I need to continue, to ultimately help others and myself. I call Kathy to schedule the mammogram and ultrasound study and strongly suggest to her that I find out the results on the same day. She says the best she can do is schedule me for the mammogram on the following Tuesday and the ultrasound the next day. I agree to that.

I arrive at the hospital at noon on Tuesday for the mammogram. Kathy comes into the exam room and tells me there has been a cancellation and asks if I can stay for the ultrasound today. I have to be home by 2:45 p.m. for the school bus. It can work. The radiologist starts to do the ultrasound of my breasts and I ask about the radiologist from the Midwest who did the ultrasound last December. She tells me she is no longer with the hospital. Interesting how that works out.

*

After the radiologist is done, I have a seat in the waiting room. Kathy approaches me and tells me that the mammogram is normal, but that the radiologist wants to see me. Keep in mind that abnormalities can only be seen on 50% of mammograms. Next Kathy takes me to the room where the radiologist is looking at my results from the ultrasound. The doctor says she sees a nodular in my right breast. I ask her to show it to me on the film and then I ask her if she thinks it is a cyst, a false positive? She says no and shows me another area in my breast where there is a cyst. She stands up from her chair and takes me by the shoulders and says that because I am in the study, they will do a biopsy faster than normal. I ask when that will be, and she says next Tuesday or Wednesday. I tell her I am going to go upstairs to see if Dr. Ryan is in. Dr. Ryan is not in, but Pam her nurse is and takes me into an exam room and I tell her about the ultrasound results. I tell her I am not willing to wait until next week for the biopsy and

I will gladly sit in this room until she arranges a biopsy for today or tomorrow. I call a neighbor so my kids are being met at the school bus and I have plenty of time to sit and read my book. What am I thinking? I can't concentrate on reading, but I wait while she sets up the biopsy. Twenty minutes later Pam walks back into the room and tells me that the biopsy is scheduled for tomorrow morning at 9 a.m.

David doesn't answer his phone; I know he has meetings all afternoon. I don't want to alarm him, so I leave a message to call when he can. I call my friend Claudia and tell her how lucky I am to be part of the breast ultrasound study, because of the doctor finding a nodular in my right breast that is six millimeters, and that cannot be felt with the human hand until it is at least 1 centimeter, and even then that is so small it is hard to feel. I am going to have a biopsy the next morning. She tells me she will never forget my call and how good I sound about the findings and how positive I am.

I arrive home and my next call is to Judy, Dr. Ryan's office manager and surgical coordinator. I think I know the answer to this, but I ask the question anyway. If I choose to have bilateral mastectomies will my insurance pay for the whole thing, considering my left breast is the unaffected one? She says yes, the insurance company will pay for a prophylactic mastectomy, which means to remove one or both breasts to reduce the risk of developing more breast cancer. I thank her and now have to wait for the biopsy and the result.

While waiting for the result, I already make up my mind. I do not want to go through this year after year, and after sitting in that radiation waiting room and hearing the stories from other women, I know what has to be done. Dr. Ryan calls the following Thursday. She tells me that Judy shared with her that I am considering a bilateral. She tells me my other option, which I already know. I can do a lumpectomy; however, I cannot have radiation again to the same breast. Dr. Ryan knows me pretty well by now and knows how assertive I am about my health. I tell her I want to schedule the bilateral mastectomies. She gives me the name of two plastic surgeons. She says one has a better bedside manner; otherwise, they are both great surgeons.

*

It is the second week in December. With the holidays approaching, neither plastic surgeon has openings until January. I ask to speak with the person who schedules the surgery at Thomas Brandt, MD's office. Lorraine is her name and she takes my call. I tell her Dr. Ryan wants me to see a plastic surgeon for a consultation and that it will help me enormously if I can see Dr. Brandt before the end of the year. She says she can't promise me anything, but will ask him and call me back before the end of the day. The phone rings ninety minutes later. Lorraine says Dr. Brandt is willing to see me next week. I can't find enough words to thank her and start to cry with relief.

The other plastic surgeon is the one with the better bedside manner, but after going through my kidney surgery just four months before, I know what matters, it is really the surgeon's skills and expertise not their personality.

*

Dr. Brandt comes into the room. He doesn't smile once and I live with it. He already knows why I am there; Dr. Ryan had sent over my medical history prior to my appointment. Dr. Ryan suggested skin-sparing mastectomies and Dr. Brandt agrees. In this type of surgery, the breast surgeon removes only the nipple and areola and then removes the breast tissue. The remaining skin provides the form to accommodate an implant. Then the plastic surgeon inserts the implant and re-creates the nipple from skin from one of three places. Dr. Brandt explains, the first option is TRAM, which stands for transverse rectus abdominis muscle, in other words, tissue from the abdominal area. In my case I don't have any extra there, so that is out. The second option is a latissimus muscle flap. Dr. Brandt examines my back and asks me if I have had a substantial weight loss. I tell him I lost twenty-five pounds four years ago. He is happy to hear this. He asks me if I realize I have extra skin in my lats from the weight loss and it will be perfect to reconstruct the front part of my breast. He tells me the third option is to use part of the glute muscles, but that is sometimes problematic and not as successful as the other options.

Dr. Brandt explains further. Once Dr. Ryan completes her part of the surgery; he will insert the implants and use some skin from my back to create new nipples, all in one operation. Usually there will be a second surgery to create the nipple, but he feels because I am thin and in such good physical condition, he will be able to do it all in one surgery. He says the advantage of this surgery is that it requires just one operation; whereas, tissue expanders can require four to five surgeries. He also says skin-sparing mastectomy will leave me with more natural looking breasts.

I make it quite clear to Dr. Brandt that my biggest concern is eliminating the cancer. And that I worry about being put under anesthesia many times, which tissue expanders require, so I am glad that, instead, the whole process can be completed in one surgery. I am curious what size implants he plans to use. At my highest weight I am a 36B, and after my weight loss I am barely a 36A. He tells me because my right breast has been radiated that the skin will not be as supple and will not stretch as well as the skin of the left breast, so he says I can count on a B cup. Fine with me.

*

The end of January is when both surgeons can coordinate their schedules. David and I arrive at the hospital on the day of surgery at 6:30 a.m. We go straight to the surgical desk and they tell me Dr. Ryan wants me to go to the nuclear medicine department. That seems odd; she has not said anything about it to me.

They page Dr. Ryan and she explains that the doctor in the nuclear medicine department needs to inject dye into my right breast, which will migrate to the sentinel lymph node; there will be six to eight injections. She explains that the sentinel lymph node is like the queen bee in a beehive. The procedure is quite new; they have been using this technique for the past few years. By taking just the sentinel node, it helps the doctor know if the cancer has spread. In the past, the surgeon had to remove at least 10 lymph nodes, which can put the patient at risk for lymphedema (a swelling that generally occurs in one of your arms or legs).

I am unhappy that I do not know about this procedure in advance. Dr. Ryan tells me she thought she told me about the injections. It is a curveball that I don't need right now. Dr. Ryan says that David can come with me. I am lying flat on the table and David is holding my left hand. The doctor says he is going to use eight injections, to be sure that there is enough dye to move to the sentinel lymph node, so that Dr. Ryan can find it easily during the surgery, in order to remove it.

I close my eyes. I do not want to see the needle enter my breast. Each time he injects me I squeeze David's hand as hard as I can. The pain is excruciating. This is the first time I can say that the pain is unbearable. By the fifth injection, David says he is feeling dizzy and thinks he is going to faint. Two nurses run to him and help him sit down, and they take care of him, while the doctor inserts the last three needles. David says that what makes him feel sick isn't watching the needle insertion in my breast, but the look of pain on my face.

Finally we are done in the nuclear medicine department and we walk back over to the surgical wing. Dr. Ryan is waiting for me and she walks me to the gurney where they start the IV. They ask David to wait outside and will call him in right before I go into surgery. The same anesthesiologist is there, for my third breast surgery. But this one is far more extensive and serious than the first two. The minute I see him, calmness comes over me. Trust has never been my strong suit, but now is the time to put my total faith in this surgical team. And I do. Everyone on the team cannot be more comforting, and after all, I am not a stranger to operating rooms. David insists he came in to kiss and hug me before I went in, but I don't remember.

It is an eight-and-a-half-hour surgery. Dr. Ryan does her part first and then Dr. Brandt does the reconstruction. I wake up in recovery and the first person I remember seeing is Mario Russo, MD, my friend's husband. I'm sure that Dr. Ryan and Dr. Brandt have seen me as well, I just don't remember that. Mario is a friend. His wife Julie is one of my best friends and she tells me later that Mario insisted on looking in on me. He is the Vice Chair of Clinical Anesthesia. He holds my hand and asks me how I am doing. I say I am doing great now that he is there. Mario stays with me until the staff takes me to my room. I tell him I have spoken with Judy in Dr. Ryan's office about possibly getting a private room, because things did not go too smoothly after my kidney surgery. David has plans to stay with me the whole time. Mario thinks that is a fantastic idea and checks to see if indeed I have a private room. He says I do and they will be moving me to it in a matter of minutes. He says to hold on, he is going to get David from the waiting room. There is no question I am so fortunate having wonderful and caring people surrounding and supporting me.

I have not lost my sense of humor for even a moment, and it doesn't hurt that I have plenty of pain medication to keep me comfortable. The orderly who wheels me up to my room asks me if I can lift up and move onto the hospital bed. I laugh and say I haven't been doing all these core exercises with my dear friend Fiona for nothing. I lift up and scoot over to the bed. They all clap. You might think it is something really special. According to the nice orderly it is.

*

Now it is time to start recovering. The nurse puts those same inflatable boots on my legs that I've had before. I have drains and tubes coming out of more places than I want to count. This time we decide not to have the kids visit me at the hospital. Plus, David has taken the time off of work and the kids are staying at friends' houses. It is late in the day. The nurse orders a cot for David and offers him greens to wear to sleep in.

Dr. Brandt says I will be in the hospital for three days at most. He comes to see me often, at least three times a day, with his entourage of interns and residents. Dr. Ryan visits every day as well. I am always so happy to see all my doctors, and I tell Dr. Ryan how good I feel and how thankful I am that she is my doctor. She says that she has never met a patient with my coping skills. My life experience has certainly given me these skills.

Dr. Brandt is watching some bleeding from the incisions on my left breast. They watch it very closely, and on two occasions think I might have to have additional surgery. That turns out not to be necessary, but I have lost so much blood that I need a transfusion of two pints of blood. And they only allow the use of blood from their blood bank; no outside donations that are for specific patients, so David cannot donate blood in advance for me. I so appreciate the silent heroes who give their blood. Once again, I have to put my faith in Dr. Brandt, and if I need the blood that is the way it is. I end up in the hospital for five days. Beautiful flower arrangements keep coming from family and my wonderful friends.

David does not leave the room once. When I need a nurse, I push the call button, but he is always at my side helping make me more comfortable before the nurse arrives. I know that if I look up the word devotion in the dictionary, without a doubt David's picture is there. His patience and concern for me have no limits. I never forget this.

*

When it is time to go home they remove the IV and catheter, but I need to keep the surgical drains that are in the incisions in my back and under my breasts.

I am not able to drive for a while. My friend Alexis takes me to my follow-up appointment with Dr. Brandt, which is two weeks after the surgery. He says it is time to remove the drains. It is painful, but far more bearable than the injections of dye. He says I need to return in a week for another checkup.

Over the weekend two major things happen. One, I notice a bulging of skin on my back, right under where the drains were. I call Dr. Brandt. He isn't on call that weekend, I speak to one of his associates who tells me it is cirrus fluid building up, because I no longer have drains. It is common but does not occur all the time. He says he will inform Dr. Brandt and I can see him on Monday.

The other news is a call from Dr. Ryan, telling me she has great news, and other news. I hold my breath. She says that I have stage 1 cancer in the right breast, and the sentinel node shows it has not spread to my lymphatic system. This is good news. The other news is that the pathologist finds 2 millimeters of invasive lobular cancer in my left breast, near my cleavage, the breast that I think is free of cancer. That means that the cancer cells break out of the lobule and have the potential to spread to other areas of the body. It is the least common type of breast cancer. It does not usually appear as a lump, but instead causes a thickening of the tissue or fullness in part of the breast. Another way to put it is that it hides and is not easy to find, until stage 3 or stage 4 breast cancer. Dr. Ryan insists that I consider a second surgery the following Tuesday to remove lymph nodes under my left arm to assure the cancer is not in my lymphatic system. Once again, my head is spinning. David is not home from work yet when Dr. Ryan calls. I tell her I will need to speak to him and get back with her.

That night, David and I go to work searching the web for information. What we both come up with is that there are higher risks of developing lymphedema if I have the surgery than of the cancer being in my lymph nodes. Lymphedema is a side effect that can begin during or after lymph nodes are removed under the armpit. It isn't life-threatening, but can last for a long time and is often not reversible. It involves swelling of the tissues of the arm and sometimes the hand. The swelling can cause discomfort and become a chronic problem. I call Dr. Ryan back and tell her about our findings, that David and I have to think about it for a while, and that I am not going to agree to another surgery right now.

As luck has it, the next morning I have an appointment with Dr. Brandt. I tell him everything Dr. Ryan told me and he gets angry and says exactly what David and I already know. He says there is far more risk for me to end up with lymphedema, even if it doesn't occur immediately after the removal of the lymph nodes. And now there is no breast tissue left for Dr. Ryan to find the sentinel node, so she proposes to take half my lymph nodes, which is about 20. Dr. Brandt says I could wake up with a swollen arm, anytime, in a week, a month or a year. Another surgery is far too dangerous, and he adds I already have enough chronic illness to handle. And the likelihood that the 2 millimeters of lobular cancer have been able to reach my lymphatic system is very low.

I am ecstatic about his reaction. And he promises me he will contact Dr. Ryan, along with a new oncologist I will be seeing. This is highly unusual to have a doctor become my advocate and be willing to take on the whole team of other doctors, including Dr. Ryan, the radiation oncologist and the new oncologist. He tells me to go home and wait for his call and that under no circumstances should I agree to the surgery.

It is tough. I am getting phone calls from Dr. Brandt and Dr. Ryan. Dr. Ryan tells me she has a consult with a new oncologist for me. Her name is Barbara Harris, MD. Dr. Ryan tells me Dr. Harris is not taking new patients, but she agrees as a favor to see me. David and I are going with Dr. Brandt's suggestion to not have the surgery. However, I have a consult scheduled with Dr. Harris the oncologist. I will see what her thoughts are.

I have a ninety-minute consultation with Dr. Harris. I have come in with my notebook, the same one I take with me to all my appointments. She tries to convince me to have the surgery to remove the additional lymph nodes under my left arm.

I am done with all these doctors pushing and pulling at me. I tell her that with Dr. Brandt's guidance I am not having surgery to remove any more lymph nodes. I ask her anyway, off the record, that if she was me and considering all my health concerns, would she agree to the surgery? She pauses and looks up at me. It takes her a moment then she says, "NO." I write that down in my notebook and ask her to sign it and promise I will not share the information with Dr. Ryan.

Dr. Brandt calls me two days later after all four of the doctors have sat down to discuss my case, Dr. Brandt tells me he wins. There is not going to be another surgery.

What a relief. Dr. Brandt is my hero. I do have a long conversation with Dr. Ryan, as this is the first time I adamantly disagree with her advice. She says she understands how I came to my decision and she will support me.

*

The next week it is time to see Dr. Brandt again. I go to a lingerie store beforehand, because I am ready to get out of the special compression bra I have been wearing since the surgery. I am one of the lucky ones, because Dr. Brandt understands how I feel about anesthesia, and that it is safer to have fewer surgeries, so he is able to construct my new nipples during the 8½ hour surgery, which is usually not always doable, especially with tissue expanders, which require many surgeries. A saleswoman measures me for a bra and she says I am a 34C. I say that can't be, that my plastic surgeon says the biggest I will be is a B cup. She helps me try on 34B and 34C bras and she is right, I am a 34C.

It is always fun for me to make Dr. Brandt smile. I crack jokes and let him know he has to smile each time I have a visit with him. I tell him about my bra shopping experience. He asks how I feel about it. He says most women are happy to be bigger breasted. I tell him it isn't that I am unhappy, just that it is quite an adjustment for me going from barely an A cup to a C. I have to give my daughter all my tops and sweaters, because nothing fits me anymore, and I keep bumping into walls, my breasts are protruding so much and taking up more space. He has a belly laugh and gives me a hug. Wow, a hug!

When we stop laughing, he tells me that he is extremely happy with my healing progress. I ask him why I am healing so quickly.

He says there are three reasons. For one, I had extra skin on my lats, so less stretching of the skin was necessary. Plus, I am thin, and I have a great outlook!

*

My next visit is with Debbie, Dr. Brandt's nurse, to tattoo my new nipples, because my whole breast is the color of my skin, with only a mark of where the nipples were surgically built. I am not too sure about this. Why do I care either way? She convinces me that once it is done, I will be happy with the result. Like anything else, it is a process. She and I pick the color together then she does the tattooing. I have to leave gauze over the tattoo for a week. Debbie is absolutely right. Now if anyone at the gym sees me getting my clothes on after my shower, I no longer have just two bloops on my chest; the nipples look natural. It is the best thing I do to complete the new me.

*

I do physical therapy to make sure I have not lost any range of motion in my arms and shoulders. Many women who have had the same surgery as me recommend it, and Dr. Brandt is happy to write me a prescription for it. I continue to heal, though during the first six months or so, I have a lot of tenderness from the scars on my back. It is true that my bra straps cover the scars on my back, but if anyone knocks into me with their handbag or backpack, I have a sudden wave of pain. Otherwise, I have no complaints.

I have heard from other women and my doctors that I obviously will no longer have nipple sensation, since they are gone, and that my breasts will feel numb. None of this concerns me, or David for that matter. Our only concern is that the cancer is gone and that I have made the right decision to have the bilateral, which I believe I have. Dr. Ryan tells me the statistics are 40% or higher that if you have breast cancer in one breast in your lifetime, the other breast will eventually become cancerous too.

Each day I grow stronger. My good friend Kim insists I start doing energy work and visit the Eastern side of the world for guidance in healing. I fight it for a while, working in the Western medical world and being a patient as well. Kim has many fine qualities, especially her nurturing side. She continues to push, and I know all of her advice is full of love for me and my recovery. I try meditation, yoga, kundalini yoga, acupuncture and massage, and continue the exercises that have been my favorites, along with walking outside and using the recumbent bike, cross-trainer and other machines.

Then I find Tai Chi and Qi Gong. I am not a very patient person and it takes years, possibly decades, to get good at a martial art. But the benefits have been remarkable for me. I move differently, I breathe differently. I have been able to decrease my stress and my blood pressure medication, all for the better. I take Tai Chi class at least two times a week. It has become a way of life.

61

After going through my breast cancer, I know I want to help others. I have become a spokesperson for Susan G. Komen, I help other charitable organizations, and I have become a healthcare advocate. My passion is to help more and more people understand the importance of listening to your body and always being the best advocate possible for yourself and your loved ones. Never be afraid to get a second or even third opinion if you become ill. Don't be afraid to ask questions. Come to the doctor with a list of questions, which is the way to ensure you understand everything you need to know.

I diligently and tirelessly go for semiannual and annual appointments with my entire list of specialists. And because they are at three different hospitals, it remains my job to be sure that they are all aware of each and every test result. I know that God has his hand in everything that happens to me in my life. And just when I think I can't possibly get any stronger, another challenge comes my way. I feel that each and every challenge I have had to conquer is a blessing; they define who I am. And after dozens of years of therapy, I now realize that I have self-worth. In a way, life without adversity is life without growth.

Note from the Author

It is a sunny, breezy morning in Hollywood Beach, Florida. It is late December 2010, my 53rd birthday. We are in Florida for winter break, David and our two teenage children, Kate and Peter. We are waking up to this lovely day and ready for a long walk on the boardwalk; our hotel is right on the beach. I am ecstatic to be alive to share another birthday with my family, who stand by my side to support me in every way imaginable. In the past eight years, I have had six different surgeries for three kinds of cancers, and I survived them all!

* * *

If you would like to contact Elaine, you can email her at
damagedmerchandise8@gmail.com.

CPSIA information can be obtained
at www.ICGtesting.com
Printed in the USA
FSHW011424100221
78456FS

9 780578 836973